NEW
SWEDISH PLAYS

The logo of Norvik Press is based on a drawing by Egil Bakka (University of Bergen) of a Viking ornament in gold, paper thin, with impressed figures (size 16x21mm). It was found in 1897 at Hauge, Klepp, Rogaland, and is now in the collection of the Historisk museum, University of Bergen (inv.no.5392). It depicts a love scene, possibly (according to Magnus Olsen) between the fertility god Freyr and the maiden Gerðr; the large penannular brooch of the man's cloak dates the work as being most likely 10th century.

Cover illustration: *Springtime*, by Prins Eugen. Valdemarsudde, Stockholm.

Gunilla M Anderman

NEW
SWEDISH PLAYS

Norvik Press
1992

Selected Norvik Press books:

Michael Robinson: *Strindberg and Autobiography*
Irene Scobbie (ed.): *Aspects of Modern Swedish Literature*
Barry Jacobs and Egil Törnqvist: *Strindberg's Miss Julie*
Michael Robinson (ed.): *Strindberg and Genre*
Hjalmar Söderberg: *Short Stories*
P C Jersild: *A Living Soul*
Sara Lidman: *Naboth's Stone*
Selma Lagerlöf: *The Löwensköld Ring*

James McFarlane: *Ibsen and Meaning*
Robin Young: *Time's Disinherited Children* [Ibsen]
Janet Garton & Henning Sehmsdorf: *New Norwegian Plays*

Ingmar Bergman: *En själslig angelägenhet.* ©Ingmar Bergman, 1990. This translation ©Eivor Martinus, 1992.
Stig Larsson: *Röd Gubbe.* ©Stig Larsson, 1991. This translation ©Duncan Foster, 1992.
Lars Norén: *München—Athen.* ©Lars Norén, 1983. This translation ©Gunilla M Anderman, 1992.
Agneta Pleijel: *Några sommarkvällar på jorden*, 1984. ©Agneta Pleijel, 1984. This translation ©Mark James, 1992.

British Library Cataloguing in Publication Data
New Swedish Plays
I. Anderman, Gunilla
839.727408

ISBN 1-870041-19-4

First published in 1992 by Norvik Press, University of East Anglia, Norwich, NR4 7TJ, England
Managing Editors: James McFarlane and Janet Garton

Norvik Press has been established with financial support from the University of East Anglia, the Danish Ministry for Cultural Affairs, The Norwegian Cultural Department, and the Swedish Institute. The publication of this book has been aided by a grant from The Swedish Institute.

Printed in Great Britain by Biddles Ltd., Guildford, Surrey GU1 1DA.

Contents

Preface

Although many contemporary Swedish plays would have merited inclusion, the four plays presented in this volume are all concerned with different aspects of human relationships during the last few decades of this century. While reflecting the prevailing mood and thinking in modern day Sweden, the issues aired in these plays are in no way unique to that country but are in many ways universal, shared by a number of Western industrialized nations.

A Matter of the Soul by Ingmar Bergman was translated by Eivor Martinus, freelance writer and translator who has recently translated Strindberg's chamber plays into English. She has also translated Swedish novels into English as well as English plays into Swedish for stage production in Sweden.

Duncan Foster, the translator of *Red Light* by Stig Larsson, studied Swedish at university level, then went to live in Sweden where he worked as a teacher and translator. Now back in England, he works as a freelance translator and an English language consultant.

Mark James, who translated Agneta Pleijel's *Summer Nights*, is also a university student of Swedish. A translator, BBC journalist and television researcher, he now specializes in European affairs.

Gunilla M Anderman, the translator of *Munich—Athens*, is the Director of the Programme in Translation Studies in the Department of Linguistic and International Studies at the University of Surrey. Dr Anderman is the author of several articles on English and Swedish drama, in particular on Lars Norén, and has translated a number of Swedish plays which have been staged in England and in the United States.

Thanks are due to a number of people for helping me to see this project through to completion. I would like to thank the individual playwrights, their publishers and their agents for their co-operation, together with the Swedish Institute for their financial assistance. I also

Ingmar Bergman

wish to thank the Dramaten (the Swedish National Theatre) and in particular its Artistic Director, Lars Löfgren, for generous help. I am also grateful for the help received from Eva Ancker of Swedish Radio and from Göran Söderlund, Director of the Prins Eugen Museum at Valdemarsudde.

GUILDFORD, ENGLAND   GUNILLA M ANDERMAN
August 1992.

Contemporary Swedish Theatre
An Introduction

The Emergence of Modern Theatre in Sweden

In the late nineteenth century Sweden was isolated. In the theatre, escapism was the rule and the interest awakened in other parts of Europe, including Scandinavia, in airing social issues on stage, largely passed Sweden by. Swedish theatre audiences did not seem to have been ready to take on board the realities of life on stage. Strindberg's naturalistic dramas such as *Miss Julie* and *The Father* failed to gain favour and Swedish theatre at the time showed few signs of initiative or innovation. Around the turn of the century, the Dramaten, the Royal National Theatre, staged a radically simplified version of Strindberg's *To Damascus*, often viewed as a precursor to modern Swedish theatre. But this proved to be an isolated event and some time was to pass before the Dramaten was to venture such an imaginative undertaking again.

On the whole, critics and audiences alike seem to have lacked understanding and appreciation of any innovative move in the theatre and, given the spirit of the first decade of the twentieth century, it is not surprising that Strindberg's *Dream Play* as well as his chamber plays remained virtually unknown. Any attempts to experiment with lighting and staging were not found at the Dramaten but at the Intima Teatern in Stockholm where Strindberg attempted to recreate the atmosphere of the French symbolist theatre which he had encountered during the years he spent in Paris. In 1910, however, the experiments at the Intima Teatern had come to an end and while in France, Germany and Russia the theatre was awash with new techniques and ideas, Swedish theatre remained parochial, lagging behind developments in other parts of Europe. In England Gordon Craig advocated a break with any form of imitation in the theatre, the director creating a visionary unity of action and word, form and colour and in Russia Konstantin Stanislavsky tried to introduce new methods of acting. And in Germany Max Reinhardt, the unchallenged master of German theatre, experimented with new techniques creating atmospheric productions which were a far cry from earlier forms of naturalistic acting and staging.

Through a series of visits to Stockholm during the early part of the twentieth century, Max Reinhardt and the young Russian choreographer Mikael Fokin put Sweden in touch with the rest of Europe. Reinhardt made, in all, four lengthy visits with productions varying from Shakespeare to Strindberg. His staging of Strindberg's chamber plays attracted particular attention and stunned Swedish audiences were shown a new side of Strindberg.

Stimulated by the developments in Europe, Swedish directors went abroad and studied in Berlin and Paris. In the spring of 1918, the young Swedish director Per Lindberg went to Berlin to follow Reinhardt's work at close range. Back in Sweden he took charge of the Lorensberg Theatre in Gothenberg. First started in 1916 under the artistic leadership of Mauritz Stiller, the Lorensberg Theatre was turned into the first modern theatre in Sweden thanks to the combined effort of Per Lindberg and his designer Knut Ström.

The breakthrough for modern theatre in Stockholm was to take longer however, and when in November 1919 Olof Molander made his debut as a director at the Dramaten, naturalism still reigned supreme at the Swedish National Theatre. But Molander, whose famous Strindberg productions started in the autumn of 1922, ushered in a new directorial era with productions characterized by a strong visual impact and new lighting techniques. About this time too, painters were invited into the theatre as designers. In the spring of 1921 the well known Swedish painter Isaac Grünewald shocked the Stockholm Opera audience with his design for Samson and Delilah, the start of an on-going co-operation between opera, theatre and artists, including such names as the painter Prince Eugen and the sculptor Carl Milles. And by 1925, Molander having led the way with his innovative productions, modern theatre was firmly established at the Swedish National Theatre.

The Inter-War Years

As the result of the increase in leisure time at the end of the war theatre came to play an increasingly important part in the life of middle class Swedes. In the bigger towns subsidized, so called City Theatres were set up, Hälsingborg leading the way in 1921. In addition to the traditional proscenium stage, a number of theatres also allocated space to new studio stages for experimental, avant-garde theatre which made it possible to double the number of on-going productions offered to the public. Like the cinema, by now widely accepted by all social classes, these studio theatres could offer small scale productions in a more intimate atmosphere, gaining them rapid popularity.

Another factor contributing to the growth of Swedish drama at the time was the Radio Theatre which made its debut in January 1925. Two years later, a competition for the best radio play met with an immediate response from a number of established Swedish writers, and in the autumn of 1929 when Per Lindberg took over as Head of Radio Drama, the work of the Swedish writing elite was regularly dramatized for radio productions. A Swedish writer at the time whose literary works were often dramatized was Hjalmar Söderberg (1869-1941), the author of *Gertrud*, a psychological study of a woman, which was later to be turned into a film by the Danish film director Carl Dreyer in 1964. Another writer, by many considered to be the greatest Swedish novelist of the twenties and thirties, was Hjalmar Bergman (1883-1931). His highly successful family comedy *Swedenhielms* had its première in 1923. Many of the dramatized versions of his novels are still highly popular, including *Markurells in Wadköping*, a tragi-comedy about small town life, one of the Dramaten's successes during the early 1990's with Max von Sydow in the leading role.

11

In 1929, responding to the invitation for more popularist theatre, Vilhelm Moberg (1898-1973) wrote *Market Evening*, sometimes referred to as one of the best crafted plays in Swedish. It tells the story of the greedy farmer Magnis, plotting to marry a rich widow but in the end having to settle for his house-keeper to avoid paying her the salary owed to her. Later in the mid-forties, Moberg was also to make an important contribution to the hotly debated question of abortion with his play *Our Unborn Son,* and again in 1958, when in *The Judge* he attacked the Swedish judiciary. To modern generations of readers, however, Vilhelm Moberg is probably best known for his historic epic charting the Swedish emigration to the United States.

When, in 1929, the Wall Street Crash triggered off a world depression, Sweden was not spared. Bad times culminated in an incident in 1931, which was to go down as the darkest moment in the history of the Swedish Labour Movement. An industrial conflict in Ådalen, in the north of Sweden, led to a peaceful demonstration. But as the result of the army having been called in, five civilians were killed and several wounded, events recorded by the film maker Bo Widerberg in *Ådalen-31*, his widely acclaimed film of the seventies.

Further unhappiness was added to the everyday life of many Swedes as the result of the so called 'Kreuger Crash' in 1932 when the 'match stick' king Ivar Kreuger died and his financial empire collapsed. However, an overwhelming victory at the polls in 1931 effectively brought the Social Democrats into power for an uninterrupted reign of over forty years. As Prime Minister, Per Albin Hansson set about sorting out Sweden's problems in industry and agriculture and started to implement the Social Democratic vision of a nation caring for all its subjects.

At the time much of Swedish theatre was centred around Stockholm and Gothenberg. In order to cater for the rest of the country The National Touring Company was created, an initiative of the new Social Democratic Minister of Culture. Its original brief was to distribute theatre productions from the subsidized theatres but, as a later development, it would also launch its own performances in an attempt to widen the choice. The needs of Swedish school children were also attended to when the Dramaten took over the responsibility for organized school performances from the private theatres.

Resistance on Stage

When, in 1934, the Lorensberg Theatre moved into a new, purpose-built building, the most modern theatre in the country, Gothenburg too had acquired its own, subsidized City Theatre. From the outset it acquired a high profile with productions such as *The Executioner* by Pär Lagerkvist (1891-1974), which, not surprisingly, in the spring of 1935 came to be viewed as a political statement. A decade earlier, as theatre critic for *Svenska Dagbladet*, one of the leading Swedish newspapers, Pär Lagerkvist had actively participated in the discussions of modern versus naturalist theatre, initiated by Olof Molander's articles in the Swedish theatre journal *The Stage*. 'Naturalism in the theatre' Lagerkvist, had announced was 'five long hours ... accompanied by words, words, words'. In *The Executioner* Lagerkvist, who received the Nobel Prize for Literature in 1951, contrasts the evil of the hangman in the Middle Ages with the cynicism and racism in a restaurant milieu of his own time. While *The Executioner* was a dramatization of one of Pär Lagerkvist's novels, *Midsummer Dream in the Work House* was written for the stage. This play which purported to portray man's dreams of happiness fighting to survive the grim realities of everyday life opened in Stockholm in 1941.

The spirit of Swedish resistance on stage however was perhaps most clearly conveyed by Vilhelm Moberg's *Ride to-night!* At a time when Denmark and Norway were both under German occupation this account of the Swedes' seventeenth-century struggle for freedom left no one in doubt about its underlying message. And in February 1944, only a month after the Danish writer Kaj Munk had been assassinated, his play *Niels Ebbesen*, the story about the Danes' fight against the German Holstein counts, was staged in Gothenburg as well as in Malmö, just across the Sound separating Denmark from Sweden.

The play had in fact opened earlier, in the autumn of 1943 at the small Dramatikerstudion in Stockholm, staged by a young director called Ingmar Bergman (1918-). The following year, only 26 years old, Ingmar Bergman was offered the post as Artistic Director of the City Theatre in Hälsingborg which as the result of the recent opening of the new City Theatre in Malmö found itself with its subsidies removed. In 1944 Ingmar Bergman took on responsibility for Hälsingborg's theatre. Only a few years later the theatre was yet again granted its subsidies.

In the forties, another director was also attracting attention, this time working in Stockholm. Alf Sjöberg (1903-1980) who was influenced by the revolutionary Russian theatre of the Twenties and the German political theatre originating with Erwin Piscator, directed a string of Shakespearian productions at the Dramaten. But he also introduced many of the new plays by playwrights from abroad with productions such as Federico Garcia Lorca's *Blood Wedding* in 1944 and, the following year, Jean Paul Sartre's *The Flies*. His great successes at the Dramaten also included some memorable Strindberg productions. His staging of *Miss Julie* with Ulf Palme and Inga Tidblad was later filmed in 1957 but this time with Anita Björk in the title role.

Peace returns

When peace returned in 1945, the world opened up again. For Sweden the war had meant cultural as well as political isolation and theatres now started to look for plays from abroad, dealing with international issues which reflected the new thinking in Europe and the United States. During the late forties as well as most of the fifties, theatre stages throughout Sweden were invaded by plays from Britain, France and the United States. As soon as a production had been staged successfully in one of these countries Sweden was usually quick to follow. In May 1956 John Osborne's *Look Back in Anger* opened at the Royal Court in London. A few months later it was available to theatre audiences in Gothenburg.

Plays by modern Swedish playwrights on the other hand seem to have attracted considerably less attention, with two notable exceptions. In 1947 Alf Sjöberg produced *The Condemned* at the Dramaten, the first play by Swedish writer Stig Dagerman (1923-54).

14

This play, together with *The Shadow of Mart*, which tells the story of a dead resistance hero and the problems his fame creates for his brother, was later published under the title *Dramas of the Condemned*. Stig Dagerman's theme, the existential 'angst' of the period, shared many features with both Pär Lagerkvist and Jean-Paul Sartre. And then there was Ingmar Bergman. Experimenting with new means of dramatic expression Bergman would sometimes produce his own chamber plays about Man caught between Good and Evil, themes which were later to become the trademark of his films.

The early fifties also saw Ingmar Bergman leave the City Theatre in Gothenburg to take up the position as Artistic Director of the recently established City Theatre in Malmö. The special demands of this theatre called for a director who would take up the challenge of putting its vast stage to good use and the choice fell on Bergman. Now an established film director of growing repute, his first production was *The Crown Bride*. In the spring of 1954 this was followed by *The Ghost Sonata*, another Strindberg production. Ingmar Bergman had seen Olof Molander's production of the play at the Dramaten in 1942 and generously acknowledged his debt to the master. 'No one, I suppose, will ever realize how much Molander gave to us, younger directors'. Now Bergman was being acclaimed as a mature master, poised to take over from Molander the role of Sweden's leading Strindberg director.

The Ibsen-Strindberg Tradition

When in 1953 Eugene O'Neill died, a number of his plays were well known to Swedish theatre audiences. Sweden had early recognized O'Neill as an important playwright in the Ibsen/Strindberg tradition and awarded him the Nobel Prize in 1936. For a number of years, however, little or nothing was heard from him. After his death, Karl Ragnar Gierow - poet, playwright and, since 1951, head of the Dramaten - approached Carlotta O'Neill expressing interest in her husband's unstaged plays. As a result the Swedish National Theatre was granted exclusive rights to world premières of *Long Day's Journey into Night*, *A Touch of the Poet* and *More Stately Mansions*. On 10 February 1956

15

Introduction

Long Day's Journey had its world première at the Dramaten, a performance which was to reverberate through Swedish Theatre history. It was also a watershed in the Dramaten's psychological - realistic epoch. Not surprisingly, the Dramaten had by now come to be identified with O'Neill as 'his' theatre. O'Neill had after all written in precisely the style and tradition the Dramaten had successfully developed, starting with Molander's Strindberg productions. As we shall see this is also the tradition that, thirty years later, was to be resumed by Lars Norén.

Decade lacking in Ideology

O'Neill's interpersonal relationships seem to have been of far greater concern to Swedish theatre audiences than political issues, reflecting the spirit of the fifties, a decade that has sometimes been described as completely lacking in any ideology. In some ways the writing of the time was a reaction against the pessimistic and avant-guardist forties. Swedish plays however were still few and far between. One dramatist whose work had already been produced in the 40's was Björn-Erik Höijer (1907-). In 1954 came his play *Isak Juntti had Many Sons*, an account of the conflict between religious puritanism and overpowering sensuality arising under conditions of extreme isolation, viewed by many as one of the classics of Swedish theatre.

During the fifties the poet Lars Forssell (1928-) also turned to playwriting. In 1956 the Dramaten staged *The Coronation*, a modern version of the ancient Alcestes myth in an avant-garde production. Later, in the sixties, Lars Forssell was in fact to become the playwright who virtually dominated Swedish stages with a number of plays on a wide variety of themes. In *Mary Lou*, a pin-up of an American radio station, he returns to the anxiety of the war years while in *The Sunday Promenade* he mocks Swedish insularity, the slowly awakening awareness of the world outside and the inclination towards moralizing. In addition Lars Forssell wrote historical plays in the Strindberg tradition which included *The Madcap*, a study of the deposed Gustav IV Adolf in exile in Switzerland and *Christina Alexandra*, the seventeenth-century queen who converted to Catholicism and left Sweden to settle in Rome. Lars Forssell's popularity was to last into the seventies and one of the Stockholm City Theatre's greatest hits of the decade was the melodrama *The Inn of the Hare and the Buzzard*. With the service sector expanding steadily and becoming increasingly more important the sixties was the decade when, for the first time, the arts were viewed as a matter of public responsibility. A planned arts policy started to take shape and as a result, public funds were made available. Individual artists and writers as well as institutions were to receive financial support and a plan for future developments in the arts was passed through the Swedish Parliament. Responsibility for the arts was transferred to the Ministry of Education where, in 1963, a special division was set up to deal with subsidies to the theatres. One swiftly implemented proposal in the sixties was public remuneration of Swedish playwrights for performances of their work, including writers of plays for children and younger audiences. Another important development was the establishment of three subsidized drama schools in Stockholm, Gothenburg and Malmö. Not only did these schools recruit new generations of actors, they also figured prominently in the increasingly heated discussion of democracy in the theatre.

In the rest of the world, however, the fate of democracy was also at stake, but on a wider canvas. Political conflict flared, not only in Europe, but in the United States, Africa, Cuba and, above all, in Vietnam and South East Asia. On February 21 1968, Olof Palme, at the time Minister of Education, headed a political demonstration through the streets of Stockholm, resulting in the US Ambassador to Sweden being temporarily recalled as a gesture of Washington's irritation. Arts and politics became intertwined, more so than during any other period of the twentieth century.

Productions offered by Swedish theatres throughout the country reflected the socio-political awareness of the time. In October 1960 Stockholm too had acquired a City Theatre, a complement and badly needed competitor to the Dramaten. As its Artistic Director, Lars-Levi Laestadius was quick to pick up new trends and ideas from abroad and skilfully introduced a number of emerging playwrights from Europe and the United States into the subsidized theatre. *The Caretaker* by Harold Pinter opened in 1961, to be followed two years later by *The Caucasian Chalk Circle*, allowing Bertolt Brecht, the Communist, to come in from the cold. Dario Fo followed two years later and, in the spring of 1966, Vàclav Havel.

One of the big successes at the Dramaten, now with Ingmar Bergman as its Artistic Director, was *Hedda Gabler*, a production that cast new psychological light on Ibsen's play. Several European guest performances followed including a production at the National Theatre in London with Maggie Smith in the title role, directed by Bergman. But his most important contribution to Swedish theatre in the sixties may have been as Artistic Director of the Dramaten, setting new goals and attracting younger audiences to the Swedish National Theatre. School performances of his productions, reduced ticket prices and an increase in actors' salaries giving the profession a much needed moral boost were all the result of his efforts. When, in 1966, Ingmar Bergman handed over to the actor and playwright Erland Josephson, Swedish theatre had acquired a considerably higher status.

In the sixties Sweden also saw the emergence of a major dramatist in the Brechtian tradition. Peter Weiss had come to live in Sweden before his big international success at the Schiller Theatre in West Berlin. Before long his *Marat/Sade* was also staged in Sweden as was his next play, *The Investigation*, the Auschwitz drama. Ingmar Bergman directed, using a court-room set, designed by his long standing collaborator Gunilla Palmstierna-Weiss. Yet another Weiss play, *The Song of the Lusitanian Bogey* had its world première in 1964 at the small Scala Theatre in Stockholm. A political revue, it was an expression of the spirit and the atmosphere of the time and emerged, more than Weiss's earlier works, as a genuinely Swedish play.

But on the whole plays by Swedish writers were conspicuous by their absence during the sixties. At the City Theatre in Stockholm they constituted less than one quarter of all productions staged during the decade. This was soon to change, however. During the seven year period 1969-76, over two thirds of the City Theatre's productions were of new Swedish plays and in 1977-78 the theatre devoted a complete season to contemporary Swedish drama.

It was towards the end of the sixties that Swedish playwrights started to reappear. Helped along by the film makers of the late fifties and the new wave in Swedish cinema, Thommy Berggren, star of Widerberg's *Elvira Madigan* and a number of other, new talented actors were beginning to shift the interest from Stockholm to Gothenburg. In the theatre this development peaked with the plays by Kent Andersson (1933-), sometimes co-authored with Bengt Bratt (1937-). Inviting the actors to contribute to the script Kent Andersson wanted to create Brechtian-style variety performances, with the emphasis on the collective rather than the individual. His first play, *The Raft*, was written in 1967. A life raft with a faded flag drifts slowly along but towards what? A satirical revue with the Swedish establishment at the receiving end, *The Raft* met with immediate success and turned Gothenburg overnight into the centre of Swedish theatre. Kent Andersson's next play, *The Home*, co-authored with Bengt Bratt, was set in an old people's home. Other well known plays include *The Sandbox* and *The State of Affairs*, again written together with Bengt Bratt.

A hotly debated issue in the socio-politically conscious climate of the sixties was penal reform. In 1971 *Seven Girls* by Carl-Johan Seth (1938-) opened at the Dramaten, a play about teenage girls referred to a Swedish Community Home catering for serious offenders. One of the few contemporary Swedish plays of the period to reach a wider, international audience, it was later staged at Charles Marowitz' theatre in London, the Open Space, as well as on Off-off Broadway.

The Seventies also saw feminism emerging as a powerful force. A Swedish play on this theme which also attracted considerable attention abroad was *The Night of the Tribades*, which airs the subject of equality between the sexes in a fictional account of a meeting between August Strindberg, his estranged wife Siri von Essen and her Danish friend Marie David during a rehearsal of Strindberg's play *The Stronger*. Per-Olof Enquist (1934-), the author, was an established novelist before he turned to playwriting with a number of critically acclaimed, literary works to his name. He has since continued to combine a career as a playwright with further works of fiction as well as scripts for television. Other plays include *Rain Snakes*, about the

Danish writer Hans Christian Andersen and *The Hour of the Lynx*, first staged at the Dramaten in 1988 and later at the Edinburgh Fringe.

In 1969 Viveka Bandler took over as Artistic Director of the City Theatre in Stockholm. Concerned to give it a different profile from its close competitor, the Dramaten, she invited a number of new Swedish playwrights into the theatre. Prominent amongst these were Suzanne Osten and Margareta Garpe who had several big successes in the seventies with plays on feminist-inspired themes. Margareta Garpe (1944-), now working independently as a playwright, had several successful productions at the Dramaten during the eighties and early nineties. *For Julia* with Bibi Andersson which opened in 1987 is an account of a mother-daughter relationship, while *All Days, All Nights*, a play about the problems of old age, formed part of the 1991/92 programme at the Dramaten.

Suzanne Osten (1944-) has also continued to work independently, as a director of films and theatre and as a writer for both media. She has been linked to the Klara Theatre, since the early seventies part of the City Theatre in Stockholm, providing theatre productions for younger audiences during the day and political revue and cabaret in the evening. As the Artistic Director of the Klara Theatre for a number of years she also paved the way for children's theatre in Sweden, helping it to achieve its present international standing.[1]

As a writer of plays for younger audiences, however, Staffan Göthe (1944-) is generally considered to be unrivalled in Swedish theatre. But he has not restricted himself to this genre. A masterful portrayer of the claustrophobic atmosphere of Swedish small town life, he also writes successfully for older age groups. One of his more recent plays, *A Stuffed Dog*, tells the story of a young boy growing up in Luleå, in the north of Sweden. Staged at a number of theatres throughout Sweden to wide acclaim it is viewed by many as one of his most popular and best crafted plays.

Swedish Theatre in the Eighties

While many Swedish playwrights would merit inclusion in a volume of plays written during the eighties, the four writers who have been selected here are all concerned with the complexities of human relationships in everyday life during this decade.

INGMAR BERGMAN (1918-)

Ever since his first appearance on the Swedish theatre stage in the forties, Ingmar Bergman's influence on theatre and drama in Sweden has continued, as head of some of the country's leading theatres and as director of several of the most memorable productions of the second half of the century.

During his early days in the theatre, Bergman would often stage his own work, plays which were usually concerned with the conflict between good and evil, encounters between God and Satan, either in personal appearance or in symbolic disguise. Sometimes, he would also draw on the world of film and theatre to provide the setting for the moral debate he invited his audiences to observe on stage.

During the period of time he held the post as Artistic Director of Malmö City Theatre, Ingmar Bergman staged *Murder in Barjärna*, one of his own plays, which dealt, characteristically, with the concept of evil, to great dramatic and at times shocking effect. Listed in the programme to the production are the following plays which Bergman had selected for inclusion under the heading of previous dramatic output:

> *Jack among the Actors* (1945)
> *Rachel and the Cinema Doorman* (1946)
> *The Day ends Early* (1947)
> *To My Terror* (1947)
> *Draw Blank* (1948)
> *Joakim Naked* (1942)
> *The City* (radio play) (1950).

Reviewing Bergman's production of *The Murder in Barjärna*, Nils Beyer, a theatre critic at the time, summed up his impressions: 'This is a very unusual, at times brilliant and, overall, dramatically effective performance where play and production merge into a complete, unified whole. This is not Ingmar Bergman, the playwright, directing his own play nor is it Ingmar Bergman, the director, putting together an acceptable play. This is Ingmar Bergman using the theatre as the instrument on which he has chosen to play.'[2]

And indeed, Bergman was soon to choose to concentrate on another instrument, this time the screen. His first screen play to be produced was *Frenzy*, Alf Sjöberg's widely acclaimed film which opened in 1944. But his international breakthrough came with his films from the fifties, such as *Sawdust and Tinsel* (1953), *Smiles of a Summer Night* (1955), *The Seventh Seal* and *Wild Strawberries*, both from 1957, followed in 1960 by *The Virgin Spring*, a dramatized version of the old, medieval ballad. The sixties saw further, critically acclaimed Bergman films including *Through a Glass Darkly*, *Winter Light* and *The Silence* from 1960-62, followed in 1966 by *Persona*.

A closer look at Ingmar Bergman's film scripts reveals a wide variety of literary styles. The published version of *Autumn Sonata*, the psychologically astute account of a mother-daughter relationship, which opened in 1978 with Ingrid Bergman, Liv Ullman and Lena Nyman, consists exclusively of dialogue while his later epic, Fanny and Alexander, is a family chronicle, written in an often witty and amusing narrative style. In many ways, this turn of the century account of Sweden may be viewed as Bergman settling the score with his previous concern with God's silence in the face of man's search for an answer, a more recent development in his work. One of his primary concerns now appears to be the problems arising in human relationships in a comfortable middle class world as in *Scenes from a Marriage* (1973). The conciliatory note which has increasingly been making itself known in his later work is perhaps most discernible in *The Best Intentions*, the fictional account of his parents' early married life, transmitted by Swedish television in the early part of 1992 and available for international cinema audiences later that year. Directed by Bille August, this film won the Palme d'Or at Cannes in 1992.

A Matter of the Soul (En själslig angelägenhet), the play by Ingmar Bergman included in this volume, is a radio play. It was first broadcast on Swedish radio on 14 January 1990 and, later that year won the Prix Italia. In the original Swedish production Jane Friedmann played the part of Viktoria and Aino Taube the Old Lady. Translated into English, it was broadcast on 'Drama Now', BBC Radio 3, in March 1990, with Anna Massey as Viktoria. The play is yet another closely observed portrait of a woman. Viktoria has reached middle age, feels lonely and isolated and is struggling to cope in a loveless marriage. She suspects her husband of having an affair but his sudden death still comes as a shock and she eventually ends up in a home. Past and present merge and fantasy and reality become blurred in this highly realistic, yet dreamlike drama.

LARS NORÉN (1944-)

Since the early eighties Lars Norén has held the position in Sweden as its most frequently performed, living Swedish playwright. An equally keen observer of human behaviour, the impact of Lars Norén's work on the Swedish stage is in many ways comparable to that of Ingmar Bergman on the screen. And, both perceptive chroniclers of interpersonal relationships, their debt to Strindberg is in turn never far off. In the case of Lars Norén, we also move in the territory charted by Eugene O'Neill, another dramatist in the Strindberg tradition. The American playwright and his family are in fact the subject of one of Norén's most recent plays which opened at the Dramaten in 1991 with Max von Sydow under the title *And Give Us the Shadows*.

When Lars Norén first turned to playwriting he was already an established poet, with his first collection of poems *Lilacs, Snow* published in 1963. More poetry followed as well as three novels - *Salome - the Sphinxes* (1968), *The Beekeepers* (1970) and *In the Sky of the Underworld* (1972). His first play, *Kingsdom Hotel* (1968) was written for television.

Lars Norén's first play for the stage, *The Prince-licker*, caused something of an uproar in its outspokenness on taboo subjects such as sex and violence when it opened in 1973 at the Dramaten. Reactions from a corps of stunned drama critics ranged from high praise to outright rejection. Lars Norén's response was silence and withdrawal from the theatre until 1980 when he returned with *Orestes*. This time the reception was unreservedly favourable and soon more plays followed which all met with critical acclaim. In 1981 *Horrible Happiness* opened at the City Theatre in Stockholm, directed by Suzanne Osten, followed by *Smiles of the Underworld* a year later, establishing Lars Norén as Sweden's leading contemporary playwright.

In the autumn of 1982 *Night is Mother to the Day* opened in Malmö and a year later its sequel followed, called *Chaos is God's Neighbour*. Both plays derive their titles from a poem by the Swedish poet Erik Johan Stagnelius. Although written earlier, *Courage to Kill* (1978) constitutes the last part of what Lars Norén himself views as a trilogy. These three plays are perhaps some of the best known amongst Lars Norén's early work, having all been transmitted on Swedish television, directed by Björn Melander.

The trilogy deals with the relationship between the different members of a nuclear family. Drawing on his adolescence and early adulthood in the south of Sweden, Norén portrays the life of a family living in Skåne, struggling to make ends meet. The time is the fifties and in Copenhagen Stan Getz is playing in concert while in the United States Caryl Chessman's long campaign for a reprieve from the electric chair has just met with failure. Norén's portrayal of the interpersonal relationships between the members of the family - the sibling rivalry between the two brothers, the discreetly alcoholic father and the strong, domineering but ailing mother is as masterful as his successful capturing of the mood and atmosphere of the period. While in the final scene of *Chaos...* we witness the death of the mother from cancer, in *Courage to Kill* we take part in the events leading to the death of the father, this time even more brutally portrayed, since it is by the hand of his own son.

Having documented his early years in the trilogy, as well as in *Stillness* (1984), Norén's more recent plays tend to focus on the now middle-aged, financially successful children of the sixties. As always his focus of interest is personal relationships, but the setting is now the eighties. The outwardly happy and contented members of the Swedish middle class confront each other and their own lives, their waning idealism having been dealt a death blow by the assassination of Olof Palme, the Swedish Prime Minister, in February 1986. Plays on this theme include *Holy Communion* (1984), *Strolling Players* (1987) and, although it involves only one couple and not Norén's usual two, *Munich - Athens* (1982).

Munich — Athens (München — Athen), the play by Lars Norén included in this volume was transmitted on Swedish television before it opened at the Soho Poly Theatre in London in February 1987.[3] The play shows how David and Sarah, cooped up in each other's company during a forty-eight hour train journey to Athens, taunt and fondle their way across Europe. She alternates between regaling him with the details of her affairs and trying to blackmail him emotionally into moving in with her. He responds by being clever and cruel. All the while, outside, in the train corridor lurks an enigmatic middle European guard, voyeuristically intruding at intervals to demand tickets and to look Sarah over, all to David's growing infuriation. The play was directed by Brian Stirner with Deidra Morris as Sarah, Jack Galloway as David and Glen Murphy as the Guard.

In *Munich - Athens,* as indeed in his other plays, Lars Norén shows us the discrepancy between verbal behaviour and physical actions, between alleged happiness and manifest inability to experience emotions. Sarah and David are both easily identifiable representatives of the newly affluent and successful middle class, suffering the after-effects of rapid achievement. And as such they do not appear to be a specifically Swedish phenomenon, as shown by the reviews in the London press after the play opened which referred to Sarah and David as 'a modern, recognisable couple'.

During the last few years Lars Norén's plays have often premièred abroad. In 1989 *Hebriana* opened in the Hague, *Dragonflies* in Kassel and *Autumn and Winter* in Copenhagen, a clear indication the Lars Norén is now becoming established outside Sweden. The style and content of his plays are also becoming more easily accessible. Whereas in *Autumn and Winter* we return to the familiar territory of the nuclear family, locked in the grip of never-ending conflict, the tone is now less sombre, the mood lighter. Like Ingmar Bergman, Lars Norén seems to be approaching the last decade of the century on a note which is close to being conciliatory.

AGNETA PLEIJEL (1940-)

In 1968, while still a university student of Swedish Literature, Agneta Pleijel started to work as a literary critic. It was also about this time that she started to think about taking up playwriting and a year later her first play premièred in Gothenburg. Co-authored with Ronny Ambjörnsson, *Order Rules in Berlin* is a Brechtian style cabaret, written in the spirit of the late sixties, a socially and politically committed account of Germany in the years 1918-1919. The play is a trial with the alleged murderers of Rosa Luxembourg and Karl Liebknecht in the dock. Who were they? Why were they let off scot free? And, above all, what lessons are we to draw from the events which took place in Germany in 1918-1919?

The political commitment which Agneta Pleijel showed in her first play was to remain but before she was able to devote herself full-time to a career as a playwright, poet and novelist she worked for several years as a literary editor for a number of daily newspapers and literary journals. In 1975 she took over from Karl Vennberg, the writer, as Arts Editor of *Aftonbladet*. She resigned in 1979 to become a free lance writer. Since 1987 she has been President of Swedish PEN.

Several of Agneta Pleijel's later plays premièred at the Folkteatern or Folkan in Gothenburg where Lennart Hjulström, its Artistic Director, initiated a number of community projects in the spirit of the seventies. Not infrequently Agneta Pleijel would contribute as a playwright and for a number of years her plays would be launched at the Folkan, directed by Lennart Hjulström, then to be moved to other Swedish stages. In 1977 they co-operated on the production of *Lucky Lisa*, a futuristic vision of a society which dictates the behaviour of its citizens with few who dare to oppose it. Lucky Lisa, played by Gunilla Nyroos, does and is taken to court for having committed the crime of being unhappy because in a technologically ruled society the state of unhappiness is a threat to the powers that be.

Two years later, in 1979, came the première of *Kollontay*, Agneta Pleijel's play about Alexandra Kollontay, the Russian envoy to Stockholm during the second world war. The play started at the Folkan, directed by Lennart Hjulström. But whereas the play staged in Gothenburg gave a portrait of a woman torn between work, love, family and political beliefs, it acquired a completely new dimension when it moved to the Dramaten in Stockholm. Under the direction of Alf Sjöberg it now became a vivid exposé of the Russian Communist movement, from ideological internationalism to partial jingoism. A second protagonist emerged in the shape of the futurist poet Vladimir Mayakovsky and as Kollontay's dreams of freedom are crushed by Stalin so are Mayakovsky's hopes for creative freedom for the arts.

Agneta Pleijel's co-operation with Lennart Hjulström continued when she turned to screen writing. In 1984 he directed her film *The Dark Hill of the Moon* about the famous Russian mathematician Sonia Kovalevski who became the first woman professor in Sweden at the end of the last century. As in Kollontay, the film focuses on the problem of a professional woman trying to combine a career with the duties of a wife and mother. Agneta Pleijel has also written scripts for television. Notable among these is *The Golden Cage* (1991) directed by Björn Melander, which tells of an immigrant woman whose child is removed by Swedish social workers as the result of alleged sexual abuse.

Agneta Pleijel is also a poet and in 1981 her first collection of poems was published, under the title *Angels, Dwarfs,* followed in 1991 by *Eyes From a Dream.* In addition, she has written two novels. *He Who Observeth the Wind* was published to wide acclaim in 1988 and won the Esselte Prize, a major Swedish national award. It is an account of childhood memories and in particular of her grandfather who went to live in the Dutch East Indies at the end of the century. In *Dog Star,* (1989), which takes its title from the brightest star in the universe, Agneta Pleijel's latest novel, she gives us the fantasies and experiences of a young girl approaching puberty.

Summer Nights (1984) (Några sommarkvällar på jorden), the play by Agneta Pleijel included in this volume, premièred at the Folkan in Gothenburg before it was staged at the Dramaten in Stockholm and, in 1987, was turned into a film, directed by Gunnel Lindblom. The play tells the story of three sisters, all very different, and their husbands who meet for a couple of weeks every summer, in the summer house of their childhood. Chekhov's three sisters, yes, but in this Swedish version they have all escaped to the big city. But at what price? Agneta Pleijel asks questions about present day relationships. Can it work if the woman is older and can't have a child? Can a woman survive as an artist while remaining a mother and wife? The play encapsulates all the important issues we now face and will continue to face as we approach the next century.

STIG LARSSON (1955-)

Although there is a literary tradition depicting violence in a hard-hitting non-moralising style, with proponents such as Ernst Jünger, Norman Mailer and Yukio Mishima, this phenomenon has only surfaced in Sweden during the eighties. One Swedish writer of the new generation perhaps most clearly exemplifying this trend is Stig Larsson, the youngest Swedish playwright to contribute to this collection of new Swedish plays. In many ways, Stig Larsson is the forerunner of a new generation of Swedish writers for whom exceeding the limits of bourgeois decency has become something of a fetish. The tendency may be viewed as related to the avant-garde tradition of the twentieth century according to which anything is permissible as long as it is genuine and enriches our experience.[4]

The most unsettling aspect of Stig Larsson's writing is perhaps its combination of seemingly superficial trivia and shock-inducing elements. Light conversation and internal monologues figure prominently, only to be interrupted at a moment's notice by extreme physical or psychological violence. Stig Larsson started as a poet and writer and his technique is perhaps most clearly illustrated in one of his recent novels, *Comedy I* (1989) which is set in the near future. The protagonist and narrator called Stig - it would be pointless to call him anything else according to the writer - has an initially promising start to his career as a writer but falls out with the literary establishment and is no longer able to publish, having to make a living from writing sketches for live sado-masochistic revues at a porn club.

In Stig Larsson's verbal exhibitionism the element of shock is of interest per se whether or not it leads to something else. There seems to be a close connection here between the scepticism prevailing in the eighties and the growing fascination with different forms of violence. In some sense it seems as if violence may be instrumental in helping to re-establish norms and, in the fragmented world which Stig Larsson is creating, exceeding limits can provide at least a temporary respite and the start of something new. Part of the doctrine is also the credo that the hero of today is the anti-hero who does not follow any rules. Virtues like honour are no longer of interest, whatever situation may arise is assessed with open eyes and any action required is solely motivated by self interest. These are the rules of the Eighties as reflected in Stig Larsson's writing. What he himself feels about it is a different matter. 'I leave it to the reader to make up his own mind' is his often quoted comment on the subject.[5]

In addition to five books of poems and three novels Stig Larsson has written the scripts for two full length films and three plays, now collected and published in a volume simply called *Plays* (1991). *MD* is in essence a play about the Swedish working class at the present time. It was one of the great successes at the Dramaten in 1987 and later reached an even wider audience when transmitted on Swedish television. The Managing Director of the title unexpectedly decides to call on one of his employees who, devoid of dignity and pride, fails to offer any resistance when his boss openly sets out to seduce his girl friend. The most recent play by Stig Larsson is *The Return of the Prisoner* which opened at the Dramaten in the spring of 1991 to wide acclaim.

Red Light (1986) (Röd Gubbe), the play by Stig Larsson included in this volume, is his first play which also completes the collection of plays in the recently published volume. Two men are waiting for the lights to change to be able to cross the street. They start talking. One thing leads to another. Or does it? As Stig Larsson would say: 'It's for the reader to decide, isn't it?'

July 1992   GUNILLA M ANDERMAN

NOTES

1.　See also Fridell 1979.
2.　Sjögren 1968, p.118.
3.　For further discussion of *Munich - Athens* and other plays by Lars Norén see also Anderman 1991.
4.　For a discussion of other Swedish writers belonging to the genre see also Glans, Kay 1991.
5.　See Stig Larsson's interview with Mats Gellerfelt. In: *Svenska Dagbladet* 17 September 1989.

SELECT BIBLIOGRAPHY

Anderman, Gunilla M. (ed) (1987): 'Contemporary Swedish Drama.' *Swedish Book Review Supplement*.

Anderman, Gunilla M. (1991): 'The Drama of the Closed Room — Some Observations on Lars Norén's Plays'. In: Garton, J. (ed.), *Proceedings of the Ninth Biennial Conference of the British Association of Scandinavian Studies held at the University of East Anglia 8-11 April 1991*, pp.24-36.

Bergman, Gösta M. (1966): *Den moderna teaterns genombrott 1890-1925*. Bonnier, Stockholm.

Bergman, Ingmar (1988): *The Magic Lantern*, translated by Joan Tate. Penguin, Harmondsworth.

Cowie, Peter (1992): *Ingmar Bergman : A Critical Biography*. André Deutsch, London.

Engel P-G. and Janzon, Leif (1974): *Sju decennier svensk teater under sjuttiotalet*. Forum, Stockholm.

Florin, M. (1982): 'Du måste förändra ditt liv.' *Bonniers Litterära Magasin*, VI, pp.392-8.

Fridell, Lena (1979): *Children's Theatre in Sweden*. The Swedish Centre of the ITI, Stockholm.

Gellerfelt, Mats (1989): 'Läsaren får själv ta ställning.' In: *Svenska Dagbladet*, 17 September.

Glans, Kay (1991): 'Våldet och fiktionen hos Stig Larsson, Magnus Dahlström och Carina Rydberg.' In: *Bonniers Litterära Magasin*, I, pp.6-12.

Gullberg, Berit (1990): *Samtal med 12 skådespelare*. Trevi, Stockholm.

Josephson, Erland (1990): *Sanningslekar*. Brombergs, Uppsala.

Linder, Erik Hjalmar (1966): 'Fem decenniers dramatik. Översikt och krönika.' In: *Ny illustrerad svensk litteraturhistoria*, pp.1007-31. Natur och Kultur, Stockholm.

Marker, Lise-Lone and Marker, Frederick. J (1979): 'Ingmar Bergman as Theatre Director. A Retrospective.' In: *Theater*, Vol.11, pp.6-63. Yale School of Drama, New Haven.

Näslund, Erik and Sörenson, Elisabeth et al (1988): "Kungl. Dramatiska Teatern 1788-1988". Stockholm.

Olsson, Bernt and Algulin, Ingemar (1987): *Litteraturens historia i Sverige.* Norstedts, Stockholm.

Sjögren, Henrik (1968): *Ingmar Bergman på teatern.* Almqvist & Wiksell, Stockholm.

Sjögren, Henrik (1979): *Stage and Society in Sweden. Aspects of Swedish Theatre since 1945.* Swedish Institute Publications, Stockholm.

van Reis, Mikael (1988): 'Det slutna rummet. En essä om gränser hos Lars Norén.' *Bonniers Litterära Magasin*, 1.

Waldén, Katja (ed.) (1991): *Teatern i Centrum. En bok om Stockholms Stadsteater 1960-1990.* Monografer utgivna av Stockholms Stad.

A Matter of the Soul

by

Ingmar Bergman

Translated by Eivor Martinus

Characters   **Viktoria**

                        An Old Woman

I

Viktoria:

I don't want to wake up. Draw the curtains again at once, I've got the sun in my eyes, I have a splitting headache. What's the time? Half past ten. Why didn't you wake me at a quarter past ten, as we agreed, Anna? You must learn to be punctual. No thank you, I don't want to hear any excuses. You're a nice girl, Anna, but you're not very good at keeping time. There... will you help me with the pillows... and put the tray over here. Oh God, my headache! I must cancel my dental appointment. Will you ring the dentist and tell him that I am ill. I don't want to make a fuss but the coffee is not exactly hot. How many times must I point out that the coffee should be piping hot? No, no, don't make any extra trouble for my sake. There is always so much to do in the kitchen and Mrs Hartwig can't think of everything.

Anna, don't run my bath yet. I think I'll lie in for another hour or so. And bring the aspirins, you know where they are... to the left of the little glass cabinet. *Don't rush*, Anna. Walk quietly. It's possible to move fast without stampeding like a bison.

I think I need two tablets. God, the coffee is awful. Give me the hand mirror, there's a darling. It's horrible to look at yourself in the mirror before you've brushed your teeth but I've never shied away from the bitter truth... that I am forty-three years of age.

Thank God I've still got all my teeth but there's one on the right that's coming loose.

But my eyes: Stupid, lazy, vacant. A *terrible* sight. Where did I put the cigarettes? I hate smoking in the morning but it's the only way of waking up. Give me a light, please, Anna. And bring me the ashtray. You see where it is, don't you? I was a very plain child, you know. My mother hardly acknowledged me, she was so beautiful herself. I was sent to a Catholic girls' boarding school and during the summer holidays I used to stay with my grandmother in Brighton. I was ugly and lonely and I cried a lot. Then all of a sudden I was beautiful and sought after. It was very confusing! Oh, it was confusing! I was the same person and yet not the same. I'll show you something, Anna. This is a picture of me taken twenty years ago. Quite an attractive girl, don't you think? I played fast and loose with the men and I *despised* them. No, that's a lie.

Why do I suddenly say things which aren't true?

I never believed in my new-found success, *that's* the truth. Oh, Anna! I feel so gloomy today. Maybe I don't want to go on living. The trouble with me is — are you interested? I suddenly thought you might be, I'm sorry, I didn't mean to sound reproachful! The trouble with me is that I am a born artist. I suppose I should have been an actress. Just think what I could have given the world. Or maybe a painter. My teacher thought I was quite talented. Far above average. There, I've finished that ghastly coffee and suffered a slice of bread with marmalade, now you can take the tray to the professor. He's probably sitting in his study reading the paper. Tell him that I absolutely must talk to him, as soon as possible, tell him it's important but nothing to worry about, he needn't be afraid. There, you can go now, Anna. I'm sorry we didn't get round to talking about you and your problems, after all. I meant to, actually.

Look, I wrote in my note-book: 'Speak with Anna about her problems, tomorrow morning first thing.' But we didn't. One needs a lot of surplus energy to deal with other people's problems. As a rule, I have that kind of surplus energy, but not today. Hurry up now Anna. I'll comb my hair myself. After I've talked to my husband I'll have a bath and then I'll see if I feel like getting up, or... I may stay in bed.

[**Viktoria** *alone.*]

Where are my slippers? Oh, terrible agony! Oh, confusion, anguish! This awful hour before noon. The final *proof*. Don't cry. Be brave to the very last. I am so *dramatic*. I work myself into such a state.

[*A knock at the door*.]

Come in, darling. Oh Alfred, you always smell so nice, what a lovely scarf you've got on. I'm sorry you have to see me in this dreadful state, but I haven't slept all night. I've thought about us and our marriage. Oh, Alfred! You're bored already. Here we go again for the umpteenth time about Viktoria's feelings. No, we're not, oh no. Be patient, Alfred. I'm going to talk about something which we've never touched upon, our *intimate love life*.

My cheeks are already burning and I'm frightfully embarrassed but I still think that you and I ought to discuss this *embarrassing* thing, which concerns us both so deeply and it simply mustn't remain a blind, nocturnal matter.

I'll sit down here in the chair behind you, so you can't see me. I've written down some questions I'd like you to answer, as honestly as you can, please. No, you mustn't walk away, you're not needed at the university for another hour. I know.

Now I'll read the first question, it's not very complicated and should be quite easy to answer. So here we go.

First question:

Why are you unfaithful to me? I can answer that question myself. You're looking for something in other women which you can't find in your wife, or maybe you're running away from something in yourself which you can't bear.

Second question:

(It's very embarrassing but all the same, or maybe because of that, it must be answered with absolute honesty.)

Second question:

Why can't you satisfy your wife with your hand?

Why do you move away when I try to guide your hand towards my thighs? And why do you get angry with me when I ask you to help me?

I could do anything for you, you know that, I could perform the most outrageous acts to please you, you know that, but you don't even want to lend me your hand for a few brief moments. Are you just as withdrawn — I can't find a better word — towards other women, or is it only I who have to lie there alone and — disappointed?

Why don't you answer my questions, why do you remain silent and why do you look at me in such a strange way, as if there were something wrong with me? It almost makes me hesitate before I put the third question, which is more penetrating and *much* more serious than the other two.

Third question:

In the past you used to come to my bed several times a week, nowadays hardly ever, maybe once a month. Is our marriage over? Do you think I've become repulsive? What has changed? Is there something I can do to improve our relationship? Now, stupidly, I'm beginning to cry and that's wrong. I had made up my mind not to cry, not to be emotional or torment you with my self-pity. Please ignore my tears, I don't mind them at all myself. Dear Alfred, don't go, don't go now that I've plucked up courage at last. This is really the most important moment in our married life.

Don't just stand there staring at me like an idiot.

I really don't know why I bother.

Go away, I am ashamed of you. I am ashamed of myself.

Go away and leave me alone! Forget everything I said. I've already forgotten. I've forgotten, Alfred. I have such a terrible memory and besides, I don't like bringing up things from the past. Good-bye Alfred. I hope we meet over dinner. You won't forget that we have guests for dinner, will you. Alfred, Alfred...

[**Alfred** *leaves the room.*]

[*She is alone.*]

Oh, it's already half past eleven and almost dark outside. The snow is falling gently, it's cold, I'll go back to bed, I won't bother to have a bath, I won't bother, I can hardly bother to go on living. I might as well go back to bed, it's nice and secure anyway.

A pillow under my right leg where I have a constant pain, I wonder what it could be. Oh, I am so sad, I'm sinking. What was it uncle Oscar used to say:

'Life has the value you put on it.'

I do try, I do try.

Oh, God, how I *cry*. I want to die, I want to die.

No, what nonsense is this, I don't want to die at all, I'm afraid of death, thank you very much, I don't want to die at all and yet I think about death all the time.

II

My dear Patsy, how nice to see you again! Did you have a pleasant holiday, I suppose you went to the South of France as usual, isn't it terribly hot down there? We stayed in town and took it easy all summer.

You must come and see us and have a look at my roses.

Dear Patsy, you're beautiful, you look so healthy, you must have put on half a stone at least but it suits you.

Nice to see you, Marianne! We only seem to meet at these Embassy receptions, how about having lunch together one day next week? We've got some *interests in common*, haven't we?

Please give me a ring, darling Marianne! God, I've got such a headache, you see. I can't cope with this sort of crowd but I go along for Alfred's sake, he loves parties. He is a real party person, and is especially good at charming people. Don't you think so, Marianne?

Oh Sonya, isn't this an unusually disgusting champagne, it must be cheap, I've already drunk far too much, it's because of my migraine. Have you never heard that champagne is good for migraine? Sonja, darling, I understand, you're keeping a look-out for your lover. Shall I give him a little sign, no, no, I'm ever so discreet, I realize I must leave you alone for a few minutes, I'll give you a ring on Sunday. Look after yourself, Sonya.

Oh dear Monsieur Doucet, you're lost in thought before one of my favourite paintings! I adore him, the great inimitable Eugene Carriere, I worship him.

I love his courage, his mental strength, his uncompromising contempt for the complacency of the crowd. I'm fascinated by his half light that is interspersed with shadows, his disdain for pretentiousness when it comes to colours. No one has depicted motherhood like him. He has penetrated deep into the very mystery of femininity! Look at the transparent shadow, the luminous light across the woman's face. I studied fine art once in my youth and I contacted Eugene Carriere to ask for private lessons, but he was already seriously ill by then. He died in the spring of 1906. I went on a pilgrimage to his grave, I was quite a romantic young girl, you see.

Oh dear! Where did the good Monsieur Doucet get to? I think he disappeared.

Alfred, darling, tell me, do I look drunk, I feel a bit funny, but that could be because I've got a cold, I had a temperature this morning.

I'm sorry I didn't mean to interrupt, I did *not* mean to interrupt, you carry on your discussion about political realities. I, personally, hate politics. I'm very suspicious of professional politicians.

Besides, it wouldn't occur to me to assert myself in this brilliant company.

Oh, my God, here he comes!

I didn't think he would, oh my God, I'm not quite sober, what am I to do, what if he sees me, what if he wants to talk to me. Oh my God, how handsome he is! I *must* touch him. I must talk to him.

Patsy, you must introduce me to him, you simply *must*. I love his music, he is the Greatest besides Mozart. Patsy, don't abandon me! Patsy... the false bitch! I'll pluck up courage and walk up to him. Maestro!

41

Richard Strauss! It's incredible, touching you, it's incredible! I have always thought that the world of music brings us earthly creatures closer to the incomprehensible, closer to God. We're all imprisoned in our terrible loneliness, surrounded by cruelty. Music was given to us in order that we should realize that there is a world of eternal harmony beyond our earthly banishment.

In your beautiful face, Richard Strauss, I can see a reflection of the eternal light!

God, I feel sick, I'm losing my balance, everything is spinning round, it's getting dark, I'm going to faint.

III

Daddy, dear daddy, it's so nice to sit here in your crowded, hideously untidy study. It's so nice to sit here in the wintry dusk and listen to your clocks ticking away so reassuringly. And with you smoking your old pipe and everything smelling just like it used to when I was a little girl. We talked a great deal when I was little, didn't we? We spoke about serious matters, didn't we? I mean about Death and Life and Love and God? We even talked about Reality, I think, though neither you nor I were quite sure of the meaning of reality. *How did things come to be so complicated?*

I just speak all the time and people don't answer or they just walk away from me.

No, I mustn't complain. I have no reason in the world to complain. The problem is of course that I live in a vacuum, which I fill with my dreams and fantasies. Do you know, Daddy, I write poetry, I've written almost a thousand poems in the last six years, but it doesn't help. I write and write but no one reads what I write.

Oh, yes, yes, *you* read, darling daddy, you're always so kind and give such constructive criticism. Sometimes I feel I am close to a new departure. I think I possess unusual powers, like untapped riches, I almost explode under them. I often think like that but at the same time I realize that I'm stupid, vain and proud. What can I accomplish, what remarkable talents could I have?

Are you asleep, daddy? You're having a little nap, that's a good idea. Daddy, darling, I'm going to see mummy now. Have a nice sleep.

[*She walks through twilit rooms.*]

Mummy, are you there? No. Where can she be?

[*Opens a door.*]

Mummy !

[*The telephone rings.*]

Hello. No, it's not the bishop's wife, it's his daughter. I see, that's very nice, no, I don't want to disturb my father, he's writing his sermon at the moment, could you call back a little later, do you think? Thank you. Good-bye. Yes, in a couple of hours, at around eight. Good-bye.

[*Replaces the receiver.*]

Mummy's desk. So neatly organized, dust-free, everything in its place. The diary, the photographs, the pencils, her neat forceful hand-writing.

Up-bringing. Confidence. Truth, Wisdom. No force or threats or bad conscience. Never any raised voices or a sharp tone of voice.

[*She turns round: a girl around eight, dressed in an old-fashioned apron regards her curiously.*]

And who's this little girl then? Don't be afraid. I'm not going to hurt you. I'm called Viktoria and I'm visiting my old parents, just now I'm looking for my mother, I don't know where she is.

How old are you? I guess you're eight? What a nice apron you've got on.

I'll sit down here, I promise not to say a word. Don't go!

No, she's going away! She puts her finger to her lips and tip- toes away in her stockinged feet. Now she's disappearing into the dusk in the dining-room. Gone!

I didn't want life to be as cruel as this.

I didn't want life to slip through my fingers.

[*Her mother appears in the doorway.*]

Mummy! There you are at last ! Mummy ! My dearest darling mummy!

IV

I'm about to write down something in my diary which may have been a dream. I know I didn't make it up, anyway. I remember distinctly that it was a clear and still autumn day, late in the afternoon. The park with its enormous trees and white glistening statues was dozing in the windless silence.

A woman, elegantly dressed in a green velvet suit was sitting on a bench a bit out of the way. She wore a daring hat with a veil which partly covered her face. I asked her if she'd mind if I sat down beside her. She shook her head.

We sat there for a few minutes without saying a word to each other, then the woman started to cry desperately, as if grief-stricken. I asked if I could be of any help, but she either didn't hear or she didn't realize that I meant well.

In the end her muffled sobs stopped. She whispered something to herself, probably in a foreign language, pulled herself together, straightened her dress and walked away without looking at me.

Suddenly she'd disappeared among the trees.

The sun was quite low by then and was colouring the statues and the dark tree trunks. The greenery was heavily pregnant with shades of red. The water in the river was already dark, it gushed fast and soundlessly with sudden swirls in short white frothy waves. I found an old wooden bridge and walked down some steep, slippery stone steps.

Now I was on a level with the tidal water which had formed a pond with deep black water which moved slowly and menacingly just an inch below the edge of the quayside.

An ancient wall with rusty iron rings pressed into the brickwork rose out of the depth, the top half blood-coloured by the setting sun. I was getting cold but I couldn't leave this terminus. So I stayed close to the dark oily water, while the light went out imperceptibly in a hazy dusk. There were no more tears, no consolation, no point of return, not even excitement or fear. I sensed a kind of dry surprise which told me soberly: So this is how it is. This is my final truth. And that truth is nothing. TRUTH IS VACANT.

I tried to say this aloud to myself but I couldn't speak and then I thought I was probably in the middle of a dream.

V

Your Royal Highness, honoured friends. Welcome to our little theatrical and musical performance.

I can't tell you how immensely happy I am to see so many members of the Diplomatic Corps here. I'm also very proud to announce the result of our efforts. The bazaar, our dance competition, Mr. Caruso's appearance and this evening's little entertainment have brought in a sum of money which far exceeds our wildest expectations. In addition, we acknowledge the generous and noble gift that Your Royal Highness so graciously donated this year and which will enable us to make an important contribution towards our needy Poor in the city Slum. My husband... where are you dear Alfred... there he is, he is so self-effacing, my husband will give a detailed account of the various figures as soon as possible and after that the audited accounts will be distributed to each and every one of our kind-hearted patrons.

[*Applause.*]

And now my dear friends, now to this evening's main attraction which I, in all modesty and with a boldness which is in direct contrast to my talent, have ventured to scribble down and also partially, compose. So I shall sit down at the grand piano and ask for the curtain to be raised — or rather drawn.

[*Plays a few chords.*]

'The flutes of dawn play in an ''archaic'' landscape. Young nobles and maidens have awaited the sunrise under the protection of the leafy trees.'

[*Piano music.*]

'They have rested in the soft grass, they have embraced each other chastely in slumber.'

May I just offer an explanation here:

In the fifteenth century, it was customary for young men and women of Brabant to meet on a summer's night in the meadow, just outside the town wall. This one and only night.

[*Piano.*]

'...this night of merriment, hot lips, burning cheeks and bitter tears. Oh, youth, beauty, virtue, hopes, passion and despair! I'm your good fairy, I'm protecting you, I'm safe-guarding you. Nothing unclean will befall my little ones this morning. No dirty thoughts, no coarse words or ambiguous jokes are going to overshadow your happiness. I hold my hand over you all, I love you. Your passion is my perfume.'

Where are you going, Alfred? I can see you all right. And where is Marianne?

You, all of you who sit here with your mouths wide open, you knew that Mrs. Marianne Feuerkampf was fornicating with professor Alfred Egerman. You knew about it and you whispered and giggled because you thought I was an old fool and it served me right! Let me go, for Chrissake. I'm not going to kill her, but I'm going to give her a lesson, the bloody bitch. What's the matter? What's happened? Alfred! You're just joking. You're just pretending, because you want to frighten me! Alfred! He's dead.

VI

Hold my hand, uncle Oscar. Anna, help me with the dress, something has got stuck. How do I look, I think black suits me, don't you, Anna? Oh, Anna, everything is so awful. No, I must restrain myself. I must be in control.

Uncle Oscar, I'm ready now. There, let's link arms. Anna, you can walk a few steps behind me, I mean in case I should suddenly feel faint. You've got the smelling salts handy, haven't you? Good. Let's go, then. There, uncle Emil, will you open the door, please. God, how many people, how warm it is, what a smell, what is that nasty smell? Is it Alfred, it can't be, can it? If that whore Marianne has had the nerve to turn up here I'll kill her. There is Patsy, what's she got on! Her false teeth glimmer terribly in the sunlight.

It's horrid. They should have nailed the coffin down and taken him to the chapel straightaway after embalming the body. What have they done to you, poor Alfred, have they put cotton wool in your cheeks, why, it looks ridiculous! What kind of strange smile is that you've got, you never used to smile like that when you were alive. Everyone expects me to kiss your forehead now but I can't do that. God, this stench, these flies and this heat! As you may see, my dear Alfred, I'm quite calm on the surface. As you may hear, Alfred, my voice is perfectly calm, but I have to swallow my saliva all the time. Because your smell makes me feel sick.

I've never stood before Death's Majesty, the insoluble mystery before. My dear Alfred, from having been a bounder and a bully in your life-time you've now turned into a Mystery through Death.

I know people are blaming me for your death. No, leave me alone, uncle Oscar. Don't disturb me. I'm talking to my husband. For the first time in our twenty-year marriage he'll have to listen, he can't get out of it. No, uncle Emil, stay where you are, the rest of you too, stand quite still, this is going to be most embarrassing, but it's you who wanted it like this. I begged you to spare me this sight, but no one listened to me.

The depth, the breadth, the enormity, the abyss, the totality, the secret dimension can never be expressed either in words or deeds. If, instead of swallowing my saliva all the time I were to spit in your face instead, that would be just a poor demonstration of what I really feel like doing.

You lie there in your elegant morning suit and your neat patent leather shoes, with your hair nicely done and snobbish as usual, but *you've got a stupid grin on your face*. It serves you right. If you could see yourself now, and maybe you can, you'd be very embarrassed. Your smiles were never stupid, dear Alfred, never stupid, oh no, that's for sure. Your smiles were always charming, wicked, cruel, scornful and superior. Sometimes I wonder whether you were ever alive or whether you were dead long before your death.

Poor Alfred, I feel a little sorry for you anyway. I think with dismay of how you were always forced to be you, Alfred, once and for all doomed to play your terrible part. Now I can see — now when you're lying there so exposed, a victim of the art of embalming — now I can see that it would have been simple enough to unmask you.

Alfred, it would be interesting to see what's hidden behind that mask. Alfred, now I'm going to pull off your mask, show me your real face.

VII

Can you see the evening light on the snow-capped Matterhorn! And the cloud that stands out like a column of smoke from the red mountainside. Isn't it overwhelming! Anna, tell me that you too find this overwhelming!

Just being able to make a journey like this. Uncle Oscar and uncle Emil are really generous to pay for this trip and our stay at the Rest Home in Lugano.

Alfred always used to say that uncle Emil was stingy, I don't think so at all, this Rest Home is supposed to be terribly expensive, a real luxury hotel. They have doctors and nurses and all sorts of baths and treatments if you feel like pampering yourself.

Anna, my dear friend, aren't you happy? We're going to stay at this Rest Home for several months and just take it easy and allow ourselves to flirt a little with attractive men. Did you see the two gentlemen in the next compartment by the way? Very handsome and interesting-looking young men, well-dressed and well brought-up. Shall we make their acquaintance later? 'Skål', Anna!

When I was young I used to be afraid of tunnels, but I'm not any more, not so much anyway. Now we're deep inside a mountain which towers above us several thousand metres. I must laugh! I must laugh, when I think of these last few weeks, despite all the sad things that have happened.

Can you understand what got into my head, when I tried to pull poor Alfred out of the coffin, I almost tore his ears off. It would be interesting if he came back as a ghost, don't you think? I'm very interested in spiritualistic seances. I once worked as a medium. I must be an unusually gifted person! I don't say that in a boastful way, I'm just stating an objective fact... that nature has endowed me with great talents. One day I'll be able to use my talents, I'm sure of it. I'm waiting to be called, you see, dear Anna. I want to serve God with devotion. I'll be granted permission to forget myself because I'm entered in God's plan. Gosh, I'm getting very pompous, aren't I? 'Skål', Anna. Let's drink up, shall we? We've drunk a whole bottle, it's all gone, I think I'll better lie down for a while. I suddenly feel very tired, do you think it could be the champagne?

There, that's nice, here is my lovely pillow and my cosy blanket. You're a good person, my dear Anna, you're my loyal friend and I'm yours. You're so patient with your stupid old Viktoria. Oh yes, I'm getting old, it's no good denying it, it doesn't frighten me in the least. Now I'm almost asleep. Now I'm asleep.

VIII

Shouldn't we open a window, it's terribly hot in here. One can't call this view particularly stunning. No, I'm sorry, Sir. I don't allow any physical contact. You find that surprising, perhaps? You think that a woman who allows a strange man to make advances to her on a park bench — a woman like that has already compromised herself.

You think that a physical union is the logical conclusion to such an act? No, my dear friend, I beg you to keep your blazer on, I earnestly beg you to button up your trousers. 'Skål', whatever your name is.

Let's sit down here on the sofa and while away a few hours with some pleasant chat. No, I said, no. Don't you dare touch me. Now you've stained my blouse with your sweaty hands. My poor innocent white blouse. Maybe it's ruined forever.

I'm sure you wonder why we're sitting here in a shabby hotel room: you a simple beer-smelling worker from the lower classes and I a lady of the world. What was I about to say? Oh yes, you wanted an explanation why I initiated this meeting. I am an actress, you see. I'm just about to play the leading part in a new play by Gerhart Hauptmann.

I play a worn-out working-class wife who is married to a poor weaver, a terribly ordinary man who beats her, deceives her and makes her pregnant all the time. During our first rehearsal it struck me that I'd never talked to a worker, even less, so to speak, smelt one. I realized that this was a serious shortcoming on my part.

Being an actress means that you change your identity all the time...oh, correction... you're never allowed to be yourself, you always have to be someone else. It has its advantages of course — who doesn't want to escape from his own boring self? Who doesn't want to take the opportunity to forget his own grey humdrum life? I don't mind if you smoke, I don't smoke myself, I find it unattractive, I mean unaesthetic, but that's just me.

Oh, you really are desperately ugly, my dear, you are repulsive! I understand completely: on Saturday afternoons when you've finished your work for the week you first go to the pub and have a few beers with your friends, then you go to the park and look for a bedfellow for the night.

Then you'll get more drunk and finally you'll throw yourself on your poor wife, it is despicable, has it never occurred to you that you might pass on some infectious disease? Why do you smile? Was that so funny? My hair is heavy. Will you excuse me if I take the combs and pins out and let my hair down.

I think I'll take off my blouse at the same time. It's so terribly warm. I think I'll dip my arms in cold water. Will you please put the jug on the washstand. Thank you. Oh, that's lovely! There is even a clean towel here. There, I feel much better now. What about a glass of wine, the ice has almost melted in this heat, but the bottle is still cold.

May I pour you out a glass? There, let's drink a toast. A toast to the glory of work and that includes both the actress and the factory-worker. 'Skål', my dear. You may take off your blazer and cravat now.

Don't mind me, I'm sure you're completely uninhibited normally, your face radiates lechery and brutality. You're worse than an animal, an animal, however disgusting, possesses a natural innocence, but you've defiled your origin and wasted your life.

Don't come to me with excuses about your wretched childhood, your poor parents and the dirty back street where you grew up. Every person carries God inside him and every person can do something great and beautiful with his life. You, with your mortal envy of us who are better off, you wretched revolutionaries, pretentious anarchists, I despise you. So it's you who are going to take over the world one day? The working masses will bring the Paradise down to earth. Paradise where no one is superior to anyone else, where everyone is equal, where light and justice rule! I congratulate you on your simple-mindedness. Now I must tell you something that will surprise you. Listen carefully now. I'm not an actress at all, I'm not studying for a part at all.

I'm insane and I've run away from the asylum, You're surprised at my elegant appearance. It's not so strange. This is a superior kind of madhouse, the patients are allowed to wear their own clothes, it's like a luxury hotel but the beautiful park is surrounded by an insurmountable wall. The gates are locked. There are guards on patrol. Don't ask me how I managed to deceive them. I'm sorry if I insult you. It's part of the illness, you see. I don't mean any harm, it's a kind of fury which is consuming me, burning here in my stomach.

I'm sorry about all the nasty and silly things I've said. I can see that you're a good person, otherwise I wouldn't have dared accept your friendly invitation. I can see that you're tender-hearted and wise and sad. You wear strong glasses, let me take them off, oh, you've got beautiful eyes.

How strange that you've got such a good complexion, I mean considering you're always exposed to the elements. Poor man, you don't have an easy time, I can see that.

Do you believe all I say? Is it possible? But I'm lying all the time. I haven't spoken one true word during the whole time we've been together. Do you know what I am? I'm a filthy whore. A whore. It's true. Do with me what you like but you must pay me, let's see what you've got in your wallet, no, don't touch me, don't be afraid, I'm not going to steal from you. I promise that you won't be dissatisfied with my services. You see, now I'll take a little bank-note from here, the smallest you've got. Here is your wallet. You can have it back now.

This is what usually happens: just when we've gone to bed my partner, whoever he happens to be, puts on his glasses and takes his wallet out of the drawer of his bedside table. Then he takes out a bundle of bank-notes and after a long search he finds the right one. Then he hands it over to me and I immediately pull my nightie over my breasts and then he lies on top of me. It gives him great pleasure, because I'm extra willing and especially soft when he gives me a really small note.

Do you want me to take my clothes off or is it all right like this?

IX

The note-book which I'm writing in just now was given to me by Janos, one of the male nurses. We have many nurses, most of them elderly women, very quarrelsome and unfriendly. Janos is kind on the whole, he has his favourites among the patients. At the moment I'm his favourite so I enjoy certain privileges. This note-book is a privilege.

When I stuck a paper knife in Professor Jacobi's neck I exceeded the limit for what's right and proper, once and for all. That's why I've been moved to a ward for disturbed patients which is in a large house on the other side of the hill, it faces the forest. This time of the year you never see the sun, it rains and snows all the time.

We're thirty-eight patients in my ward and we're locked in two large rooms, one dormitory and one day room. All the furniture is fitted, the windows are covered with coarse nets. The lavatories are always filthy, the washing facilities are limited, there is plenty of food but it isn't very good, it makes you fat and sick if you're not careful.

Some patients are worried and keep screaming and crying for hours on end, others want to fight and make trouble. It's dirty everywhere, very dirty, it's difficult to get used to the stench of urine. Winter afternoons can be rather gloomy. It gets dark early, because our windows face north, the light fittings (we have electricity) are sparse. Professor Jacobi makes his rounds now and again, we never know when he's going to turn up. He's still got a big bandage round his neck and he sounds hoarse. Sometimes he walks up to me and looks at me but without hostility. Sometimes I try to recall my earlier life or whatever you call that strange bird-like existence that preceded my present more real life.

I try to understand what I did wrong. I ask myself a hundred questions which don't get answered because the injections make all questions futile or ridiculous. Sometimes I wonder if I ever want to get away from here at all. This sort of life can have its pleasant moments too of course, if only one stopped comparing it with other things.

Take the days when they give us a bath, for instance, the days when we get our hair washed, and when we're allowed clean underwear and clean stockings, when we're allowed to put on our Sunday frocks. They change the sheets at the same time and even though they're damp and smell of mould and washpowder, it's nice. For obvious reasons we have no mirrors in our ward, so we never know how we look. One day when I'd had a bath and washed my hair, Janos came up to me with a strange expression on his face. He had one hand behind his back and asked me if I was curious. Without waiting for an answer he held up a little hand mirror to my face. I was standing with my back to the window and the mirror reflected the daylight. I stared at it for a long time and felt a scream stirring in my stomach, but because of the injections I couldn't get the scream to surface and maybe that was just as well.

What I saw was hardly what you might call a face. I raised my hand and turned the mirror away. But I didn't say anything because speech doesn't come easily to me these days. I'm not particularly concerned about it. On the contrary, I smile secretly and think : while I was living a lie I talked incessantly but now that I'm probably living in truth I have trouble speaking.

X

I go on writing in my secret diary, and even though I've lost every concept of days, months and years a long time ago, the writing still gives me an illusion of time and something to hang on to in space.

One day they gave us contaminated food. Most of us fell very ill. I hadn't eaten so I was all right. The poor people were squirting bile and sticky muck, the floors were soon covered with a brownish stinking mess. Nurses and other staff who were called in from other wards tried to intervene but were drawn into this incredible chaos. Some were already lying powerless on their soiled beds, others threw themselves against the window nets or scratched themselves bloody against the nailed down tables. There was an icy snowy dawn in the wards, a calm merciless light. I had climbed up on one of the window-sills and hung on to the net, pressed my forehead against the sharp iron and fixed my eyes on the snow-covered trees.

In the dark forest, at a distance, I saw a beech tree which was still carrying leaves, they weren't even yellow. By focusing all my attention on this tree, by stretching myself towards the silence at the edge of the forest, I survived the unreal madness which was raging behind my back. I clung firmly to the window for several hours until after dusk. Then the storm had died down and the sick had been carried away on stretchers. Hose-pipes had been brought in and they started to squirt steaming hot water and disinfectant all over the floors and walls.

Janos took me by the hand and led me quickly and rather brusquely through a long corridor and up a flight of stairs.

He opened a door and pushed me into quite a large green room with six beds and cupboards, a high barred window. Then he locked the door and walked away. I sat down on a chair. After a short while I dared look around, at first I thought the room was empty, then I discovered a figure crouching behind one of the cupboards.

The girl was of short stature, aged eleven or twelve at the most. Her black hair was very short, she had a pale irregular face, a big nose and brown lips. Her eyes were bluish, her eyelids were arched and inflamed as if she'd been crying. She was dressed in institutional clothes.

XI

What's your name? How old are you? Why are you afraid, you don't need to be afraid. Come and sit down here on the bed. Now we can see each other thanks to the light from the street-lamp. You don't want to speak to me? You can't speak. You're mute. You are deaf and dumb. You understand what I say,though, you can lip-read? In the old days I used to be called Viktoria, but it's not a suitable name any more. What's your name? Write your name on the wall. Haven't you got a name? How old are you? Write on the wall how old you are. Don't you know? Or haven't you got an age? You're so small and thin, but judging by your eyes I'd say you've been alive a long time. Do you live all by yourself in this isolated room? Why do you live alone? Write on the wall! I don't understand. What are you writing? Princ... is it principle? Principessa? I see, you are *a royal person*, a princess, that's why you have to live in isolation. Isn't that so? Well, it's a mystery anyway.

They've turned off the street-lights outside the window. Now it's dawn. There is a storm on the way. Such a strange light, my heart beats fast, can you feel? Maybe this is the day of judgement.

'Behold there was a great earthquake and the sun became black as sack-cloth and the full moon became like blood. And the stars of the sky fell to the earth as the fig tree sheds its winter fruits when shaken by a gale. And the sky vanished like a scroll that is rolled up.'

Don't be frightened, that's just something I read a long time ago.

What are you hiding in your hand? Is it something you want to give to me? A cornelian, no bigger than a drop of blood. Are you giving that to me? You're tired, you're almost asleep. Come let's lie down here on the bed. We'll pull the blanket over us so we don't get cold. It's nice now, isn't it? We don't mind about the storm any more. The sky can unfold like a scroll, it doesn't matter either.

A little while later I was woken up by the nurses. The girl who'd been asleep in my arms was gone. They are taking me back to the ward.

The thunderstorm pushes the snow and rain against the tall windows.The sick are standing up or sitting down, wrapped in vague dreams. Some lie like blown-out candles on their beds. A sister comes with the daily injection. They also give me a bowl of steaming porridge and a slice of bread.

I sit quite still for a long time.

When I think no one can see me, I carefully open my clenched fist and look at the red stone.

Old Woman :

What have you got there?

Viktoria :

A cornelian.

Old Woman :

It's a beautiful stone. May I borrow it.

Viktoria :

Yes, of course.

Old Woman :

Is it yours?

Viktoria :

Yes.

Ingmar Bergman

Old Woman :

It's a beautiful stone.

Viktoria :

Yes.

Old Woman :

It makes your hand warm. Feel.

Viktoria :

You can almost imagine that it gives off heat.

Old Woman :

You must hide it.

Viktoria :

Yes.

Old Woman :

Our walk in the forest is cancelled. Because of the weather and because many people are still feeling poorly after the food poisoning.

Red Light

by

Stig Larsson

Translated by Duncan Foster

Characters   Jim
                        Tim
                        Tom
                        A Woman

ACT ONE

Two men are standing at a pelican crossing. The pedestrian signal shows red. One of the men is called Jim. The other is called Tim . They are wearing light summer clothes.

Jim	You don't know what it is you're saying. What is it you're saying?
Tim	I'm saying: Ouch! Ouch! Agony! Sixty minutes of pure agony. Crash! I'm saying Crash! I kept hurting myself. For a whole hour. Crash! Bang! Wallop!
Jim	Nope. That's not what you're saying. You're saying you like swimming. That's what I hear you saying.
Tim	But why do you say 'nope'? If that's what you heard, that must be what I said. But you heard wrong, you know. This 'nope' though. Where does that come from? Are you saying that I'm not saying what I'm saying? What's that all about? Very peculiar.
Jim	Now you're saying it's very peculiar.
Tim	Yes.
Jim	So I hear you all right. Have you honestly never said that you love swimming?
Tim	No. Well actually yes. I must've done sometime. But not just now. And not to you. You must've heard something I never said. I said: 'Ouch! Agony! Sixty minutes of pure agony.' I told you how I kept hurting myself. For a whole hour.
Jim	I can't hear what you're saying. You're talking too quietly.
Tim	Would you like me to repeat myself?
Jim	I still can't hear you.
Tim	*shouts* Would you like me to repeat myself?
Jim	*shouts* Yes.
Tim	Would you like me to repeat myself?

Jim	Would you like me to repeat myself?
Tim	No. Not you, *me*. Can you hear me now?
Jim	Can you hear me now?
Tim	Yes I can hear you. I *could* hear you. I've been able to hear you all the time. It was you who couldn't hear me.
Jim	There's nothing wrong with my hearing.
Tim	You didn't hear when I told you I kept hurting myself. I was rather melodramatic. I said: 'Ouch! Agony! Sixty minutes of pure agony.' I was trying to give you some idea of what it's like when you keep on hurting yourself. It was like being in a war. I kept on hurting myself. No matter what I did I kept on hurting myself. I dropped the frying pan on my foot. I tripped over the Hoover. I fell off my bike. You see what I'm saying? It was like a war.
Jim	There you go again telling me you love swimming. Why do you feel you have to keep on repeating yourself? I don't want to hear about that any more.
Tim	I love swimming.
Jim	You see, you keep on repeating yourself.
Tim	I love swimming.
Jim	Yes, thank you. I hear you. Don't you say anything else?
Tim	I hurt myself something rotten. First the frying pan on my foot. Then tripping over the Hoover.
Jim	I hear you : you love swimming. Might I now enquire as to why you love swimming? Must be absolutely mind blowing this swimming, the way you keep on about it.
Tim	It soothes my nerves.
Jim	Your nerves?
Tim	Yes. I'm a bundle of nerves. A complete mess. Crash! Bang! I'm ready to fall apart. My thoughts run wild, like a pack of dogs chasing me. But then I slip into the water. It might be the sea. Or a lake. It doesn't matter. I slip into the water and my nerves just sink to the bottom and I swim away, and leave them behind. I get out of the water and everything feels all right. A few hours later I'm a complete mess again.

Jim	Now I understand why all you ever talk about is swimming.
Tim	But I talk about a lot of other things as well.
Jim	Well, I haven't heard you.
Tim	I think there must be something wrong with your hearing.
Jim	What!?
Tim	There. You see!
Jim	I was only joking. Of course I heard what you said.
Tim	Go on then. What did I say?
Jim	I don't remember. Probably something about swimming.
Tim	No, it wasn't.
Jim	Well what was it then?
Tim	Actually, I don't remember.
Jim	Actually, I don't remember.
Tim	There. I heard you. You're repeating yourself.
Jim	You're repeating yourself.
Tim	*burps* No, that was my breakfast repeating itself.
Jim	A repeat performance.
Tim	*burps again* That's right.
Jim	Bravo! Encore! I suppose you could do endless encores.
Tim	There are limits. If you did more than a hundred you'd end up with a sore throat. Or a stomach ache.
Jim	We could always start hugging and kissing each other.
Tim	I don't think we should do that.
Jim	I don't think we should do that.
Tim	No, I agree.
Jim	I can't hear you.
Tim	There goes your hearing again.
Jim	There's nothing wrong with my hearing.
Tim	What was I saying?...Ah yes. No, I agree.
Jim	Ah yes. No. I agree.
Tim	I agree. That's what I said.
Jim	But I was being funny.
Tim	Why do you have to be funny all the time?
Jim	Because that's the way I am.
Tim	I don't think you're very funny.

Jim	What am I then?
Tim	Well, you're not funny for a start.
Jim	Well, what am I then?
Tim	What am I then?
Jim	What am I then?
Tim	You're repeating yourself.
Jim	So are you.
Tim	Damn! Am I?
Jim	There's nothing wrong with repeating yourself.
Tim	How come?
Jim	Well, sometimes the person you're talking to doesn't understand what you're saying, so you have to say it again.
Tim	But not endlessly. I said before and I say again, there are limits.
Jim	You're repeating yourself.
Tim	Yes but I only said it once. I don't intend saying it a third time.
Jim	That's good to know. Now, at the risk of repeating myself, I need to ask something. This might be the fourth time but I think I can get away with it.
Tim	Be my guest.
Jim	What am I, if I'm not funny?
Tim	You're pig-headed.
Jim	I don't understand.
Tim	You are a pig-headed man.
Jim	I know I'm a man. That doesn't exactly throw any light on the subject.
Tim	It's an expression. You can say 'Now there's a pig-headed man'. It makes it sound much more serious than simply saying someone's pig-headed.
Jim	You mean being a man makes it more serious?
Tim	Yes, it sort of gives the expression more muscle.
Jim	But I don't understand why you should think I'm so pig-headed. I don't feel particularly pig-headed...I don't like

70

the way it sounds...Pig-headed. It definitely contains negative connotations. No doubt about that.

Tim Ten out of ten for observation.

Jim Do you dislike me?

Tim I don't like your pig-headedness. But I couldn't say I dislike you. I've only just met you.

Jim Listen, my name's Jim. What's yours?

Tim Tim.

Jim All right, Tim. Now we know each others' names things can be a bit more personal. Can't you feel it? There's been a definite change in our relationship.

Tim Are you talking about love?

Jim Are you talking about love, JIM!?

Tim Are you talking about love, Jim?

Jim No, Tim. I'm heterosexual.

Tim So am I. But I thought maybe you were gay.

Jim Why?

Tim Because suddenly you looked very strange, and I thought: Here we go - love. Eh up! Watch yourself Tim. In case he tries something.

Jim Tries what?

Tim I wouldn't like to think.

Jim I wouldn't like to think.

Tim You neither. That's good.

Jim You neither. That's good.

Tim Ah! So you think like me. We're two of a kind.

Jim Eh?

Tim Two of a kind. I don't know if I'm expressing myself properly. I mean that we, as it were , think alike.

Jim We think alike, do we?

Tim Yes, in sexual matters.

Jim Completely alike?

Tim I can't really comment on that. I shouldn't think so.

Jim What do you mean by 'I shouldn't think so', Tim?

Tim Question after question.

Jim Why don't you call me Jim?

Tim   More questions. Questions, questions, questions! I don't want any more questions. Can we stop now, please?

Jim   That was a question. You asked me if we could stop asking questions. That's absurd.

Tim   It was my last question.

Jim   I see.

Tim   All right?

Jim   There you go again.

Tim   I was just checking. It was the same question: I just put it differently.

Jim   I see...No I'm only joking. Let's change. Let's try statements instead.

Tim   Right. We'll do that. You go first.

Jim   I'm in love!

Tim   With me?

Jim   That was a question.

Tim   No. It was a statement. You said: 'I'm in love!' I said: 'With me.' I stated that it was me you were in love with.

Jim   Sounds very dubious, but I'll carry on. I'm in love! I've met a woman I love. She appreciates me. We have a great time together. I'm in love!

Tim   Ouch! I hurt myself. It was very painful. Agony! A whole hour of pure agony. Ouch! Ouch!

Jim   She's called Linda. Linda! She loves music more than anything. She loves music more than me. I mean she'd rather listen to music than me. She prefers music to me. Chopin. Schubert. Piano music. Melancholy tunes. It's a problem for me. She appreciates me, but she prefers music. Music!

Tim   Music! Music! I prefer muscles. I work out a lot. I don't often listen to music. When I do it's lighter music. Pop. I like it in the background. I work out with music in the background.

Jim   Linda! Linda! As sweet as honey. She walks round the flat, singing.

Tim   I don't know anyone called Linda.

Jim   Doesn't matter. I do. Surely that's enough.

Tim   It is. But I kind of feel: 'Surely that's enough?' almost counts as a question.

Jim   Yes, maybe.

Tim   Then I can ask a question, too.

Jim   Ask away!

Tim   I haven't got a question right now. Maybe I can save it till later.

Jim   That was a question. You asked if you could save it till later.

Tim   Yes, maybe. Why can't we ask questions?

Jim   It was your idea. You thought I asked too many questions.

Tim   All right. We're allowed to ask questions again. Starting from now.

Jim   Waiting is so eerie. There are two words for every one word when you're waiting.

Tim   How d'you mean?

Jim   When you're waiting. (I've moved on to the subject of waiting.) I'll give you an example. Linda puts on a record. I wait for it to finish. If I start thinking while I'm waiting - which I do...let's say I start thinking. Then every word I think brings its opposite ... Because I'm waiting. So everything becomes positive and negative at the same time. For example. I think the thought that I want a hamburger. Then, at the same time you don't want to give up your cheese sandwich.

Tim   What've cheese sandwiches got to do with it?

Jim   It was an example.

Tim   Par exemple. That's 'for example', in French.

Jim   Good! You understand! If you think 'example' then you have to quickly think that word in French, since 'example' hasn't got an obvious opposite.

Tim   Sounds terribly complicated.

Jim   In Bengtsfors there are a lot of people living in deserted houses.

Tim	That's not possible. If they've got people living in them they aren't deserted.
Jim	That's the kind of thought it's good for us to think. If you think a lot of thoughts like that then you soon learn that's the way our minds work.
Tim	I've thought a thought that doesn't work that way.
Jim	Mmm.
Tim	I'll bet you anything that I've got bigger biceps than you.
Jim	Was that it?
Tim	Yes.
Jim	Take off your shirt!
Tim	Why?
Jim	We're going to have to compare.

They take off their shirts. Flex their muscles. Compare. Jim's biceps are larger.

Jim	Well?
Tim	I was wrong.
Jim	Right.

They put their shirts back on.

Tim	Anyone can make a mistake. But not endlessly.
Jim	Let's have another go then.
Tim	I like swimming. *Smiles.* You've heard that one before, haven't you.
Jim	When you told me that you liked swimming you actually said that you'd had an hour of pure agony. I was the one who introduced the subject of swimming.
Tim	Yes, but now I'm saying, purely and simply, that I like swimming. Nothing else.
Jim	How can I be sure of that? You might change your mind.
Tim	If you like swimming, you like swimming.
Jim	You might drown.

Tim   Yes, and if you drown you don't like or dislike anything, do you?

Jim   Precisely. Now are you beginning to understand?

Tim   I think so. But why is it important for me to understand?

Jim   When you talk to someone you want them to understand what you're saying. For example, if I were to start talking to someone who turned out to be Chinese and didn't understand a word I was saying, I'd be very upset.

Tim   Surely you'd be able to tell that he was Chinese by looking at him.

Jim   Some Chinese speak other languages. Let's say, for example, that I was blind. Then I wouldn't be able to tell by looking whether he was Chinese.

Tim   But you're not blind.

Jim   True. But I might go blind.

Tim   Yes, if you stare at the sun for several hours, but then you're not likely to do that, are you?

Jim   There are other ways of going blind.

Tim   Yes but at this precise moment you aren't blind.

Jim   It might be night-time. Dark. No lights. The sound of footsteps. I start to talk to someone. He's Chinese and he doesn't understand what I'm saying. I get upset.

Tim   What if it was Linda. Then you wouldn't get upset. You'd probably jump on her and start kissing her.

Jim   I'm not that rough. I might be upset if it was Linda. You never know. I might get scared. I might even start wondering what she was up to out there in the dark.

Tim   Now we're wandering off the subject a bit. But I think I'm beginning to understand why it's important for me to understand.

Jim   Good. You're coming along slowly.

Tim takes out his wallet from his trouser pocket. He takes out a stamp.

Tim   This is a postage stamp. I want to send a letter. But I left it at home. At least I've bought a stamp. So I can send my letter later.

Jim   So?

Tim   This is a postage stamp.

Jim   Friggy-diggy!!

Tim   Right.

Jim   Ground control to Major Tim. Can you hear me?

Tim   Of course I can hear you.

Jim   Well, why do you keep going on about stamps?

Tim   This is a postage stamp.

Jim   Oh yes look! This is a postage stamp.

Tim   Yes I know.

Jim   I know you know. We both know that...that...

Jim points at Tim.

Jim   and **Tim**   *in chorus.* ...this is a postage stamp.

Tim puts the stamp back in his wallet. Then he puts his wallet back in his pocket.

Jim   Now we've got something in common.

Tim   How do you mean?

Jim   The stamp.

Tim   It's mine. All mine.

Jim   But we've both seen it.

Tim   You mean to say that if you've seen me then you own me?

Jim   In a sense.

Tim   In what sense?

Jim   I can create whatever image of you I want. I might choose to think you're tall even though you're short.

Tim   But I am quite tall.

Jim   Yes, well then I might think you're short.

Tim   How can you do that?

Jim	Try and stop me. You can't, can you? I don't even need to tell you I think you're short. I can just think it to myself.
Tim	When you own something, you have control over it.
Jim	I have control over you. You know that, don't you?
Tim	Nope.
Jim	If I tell you to get down on your knees and kiss my feet then I wager you'll do it.
Tim	Never!
Jim	Do it. Now!

Tim gets down on his knees and kisses Jim's shoes. He stands up again.

Jim	Well?
Tim	You were right again. But that must mean that I can control you too, since I can see you.
Jim	Yes, it should do. But there are exceptions to every rule.
Tim	And I'm the exception?
Jim	Seems like it.
Tim	I think I'm going to belt you one.
Jim	You think so, do you?
Tim	Yes. I tell you I'm going to.
Jim	So you're angry then?
Tim	You might say that. Bloody livid, as a matter of fact.
Jim	You look calm enough.
Tim	Don't judge a book...
Jim	Hit me then.

Tim thumps Jim. Jim falls to the floor but gets straight up again.

Jim	So I do have control over you. I told you to hit me and you hit me.
Tim	There's more where that came from. Want some more?
Jim	I might hit you back.
Tim	Are you saying you want a fight?
Jim	No. I want to talk.

Tim   But you never stop talking.

Jim   I talk because I want to talk. That's why I talk.

Tim   I want to talk too. Who's first?

Jim   I'm already talking.

Tim and Jim *in chorus* Now I'm talking too.

Tim   So am I.

Jim   So am I. You can't stop me.

Tim   I can talk too. I'm talking now.

Jim   And now I'm talking.

Tim   And now me.

Jim   And me and me and me. A hundred million times me.

Tim looks at Jim, confused, and shakes his head.

Tim   Can't I talk any more?

Curtain

ACT TWO

Jim and Tim are still standing at the crossing. After a few seconds the pedestrian signal turns green. They cross the road which goes diagonally across the stage. They disappear stage right. The light changes again. The pedestrian signal shows red. Another man, also dressed in summer clothes, enters stage left. He positions himself at the crossing. His name is Tom. He waits for the pedestrian signal to turn green. Tim re-enters stage right. He stands on the other side of the road, also waiting for the lights to change.

Tim	Ahoy there!
Tom	Ahoy there!
Tim	It's going to take ages. It took ages last time. It's going to take ages again.
Tom	What is?
Tim	Till the lights change.
Tom	Maybe I could cross anyway. What do you think? No cars around as far as I can see.
Tim	Not much traffic at the moment.
Tom	You're going to cross over to this side, aren't you?
Tim	Yes. But I'd prefer to wait.
Tom	No cars or police around.
Tim	I'm very happy waiting.
Tom	Then I'll wait too.

They stand quietly for a while.

Tom	Lovely day, isn't it? Not a cloud in the sky.
Tim	A bit of rain would make the farmers happy. I'm thinking about the crops. It's been hot and dry for some time now.
Tom	Yes and we should think about the forests too. All those forest fires. I hear there are quite a few forest fires in the area.

Tim I haven't seen any.

Tom Neither have I, but I've heard about them.

Tim It's nice talking to you.

Tom It's nice talking to you, too.

Tim Perhaps we should introduce ourselves.

Tom No. That just makes it awkward if we bump into each other again. I've got such a bad memory for names. Sometimes I can't remember my wife's name.

Tim What is it?

Tom Will you remember it? Yes, maybe you will. Christina. Her name's Christina.

Tim That's a lovely name. What do you usually call her then? When you get it wrong, I mean?

Tom Well it can be anything really. Monica, for example. Anna, Catarina. All sorts of names.

Tim I don't suppose she likes that much.

Tom She's got used to it. She just laughs at me now.

Tim I'd really like to talk to you a bit more.

Tom Go ahead. Talk!

Tim Why don't you wait on your side, then when the little man goes green I'll cross and it'll be much easier to talk.

Tom Or why don't we do it the other way round. I'll cross over to your side.

Tim No, I think I should cross. It was my idea, after all. And it'll save you the bother.

Tom OK. Let's do that then.

Tim I think it's very easy to talk to you. I've just been with someone who was extremely difficult to talk to. In fact he was downright odd.

Tom In what way?

Tim He was so pig-headed. And he had such strange odeas.

Tom Odeas?

Tim Yes.

Tom You mean *ideas*?

Tim Yes, what did I say?

Tom OH-deas.

Tim	Oh dear. You see? It didn't take long, did it, for him to influence me?
Tom	You seem very easily influenced.
Tim	Well that was a very hasty analysis I must say. True though. I am very easily influenced.
Tom	What do you do then? For a living, I mean.
Tim	I'm a body builder.
Tom	Oh, you mean like an instructor?
Tim	In a manner of speaking. Tell me. Does it show?
Tom	I'll be totally frank. No it doesn't show. Maybe you haven't been doing it for very long?
Tim	Four years. So it doesn't show then?
Tom	I'm sorry if I've upset you but honesty is my profession. I'm a newsreader on the radio.
Tim	Really?
Tom	Yes. I'm very popular. I'm known for having a very honest voice. People feel at home with my voice.
Tim	I don't feel at home. Mainly because I'm not at home. I'm standing at this crossing talking to you.
Tom	You're only saying that to get back at me. I told you you don't look particularly muscular, so now you have to tell me that my voice isn't particularly nice.
Tim	I think you've got a wonderful voice, I just don't feel particularly at home when I hear it.

The light suddenly changes. Tim crosses. As he arrives at the other side it changes again. He hugs Tom.

Tim	I like your voice very much.
Tom	I am glad.

They finish hugging. They look at one another.

Tom	Yes, you do look very muscular, now I see you from close up.

Tim   I am glad.

Tom   Yes, you're already saying the same things as me. Easily influenced. It's true.

Tim   How d'you mean?

Tom   You said: 'I am glad.' That's what I said.

Tim   Don't you start. That's what he kept doing. I don't like it.

Tom   I don't know what you mean.

Tim   Talking about how you talk. It doesn't work if you do that.

Tom   Who's this 'he' that you mentioned?

Tim   I think I've got it now.

Tom   Got what?

Tim   Who he was. I think I've seen him before. I think he's a politician. Leader of one of the parties.

Tom   Well. Blow me down with a feather. Which one then?

Tim   Well I don't really keep much of a check on them. But I know him.

Tom   Of course you know him. You must do. You were just talking to him.

Tim   No, I know him from before. Leader of one of the parties. Actually I think you're getting more and more like him by the minute, the way you keep asking all these questions.

Tom   Politicians don't normally ask a lot of questions.

Tim   Maybe not. But he did. He wasn't a normal politician.

Tom   It'd be interesting to know which party he's the leader of.

Tim   Yes, then you could broadcast it over the radio.

Tom   Oh no. I only do the news.

Tim   Well that's news. 'Good evening. The leader of one of the major political parties is not normal.'

Tom   We have to have proof.

Tim   You are getting more and more like him...Proof! As if everything can be proven.

Tom   Are you sure you're all right? If anyone's not normal around here it's you.

Tim   I don't think you're very nice any more. I must've thought you were at first because I'd just been talking to that idiot...I knocked him down as a matter of fact. He had it coming. I didn't feel right with him at all. And I'm beginning to get that feeling again...now, with you. Seems to be catching.

Tim shows him his watch.

Tom Take a look at Mickey, his hands go tocky-ticky. Tickety-tockety, flippety-floppety...

Tim It's catching. Like an epidemic. Now you've gone very odd.

Tom smiles knowingly.

Tom I was only trying to scare you. Boo!! To get rid of your hiccups?

Tim Hiccups?

Tom Psychological hiccups.

Tim Holy hiccups?

Tom Now you've gone really strange.

Tim lies down on the ground.

Tim Yes now I don't feel normal. I'm lying down. Not normal at all. You be doctor. Tell me where the problem is.

Tom leans over him.

Tom In the head. Quite clearly.

Tim Why do you say that?

Tom That's where the thoughts are. Now I'm thinking about forest fires. The crackle of burning wood. Billowing smoke. You can't see the flames. Only smoke. Oh, but the heat. Such a terrible heat building up. Scorching.

Tim Where's Christina?

Tom Christina?

Tim Yes, your wife.

Tom   She's not there, thank God. She'd be frazzled in a flash. If she was there I mean.

Tim   I know our thoughts are up here. But I thought my problem lay somewhere else. Perhaps I ate something that disagreed with me. Some pills maybe.

Tom   Yes. Maybe. Can you undo your shirt?

Tim undoes his shirt.

Tim   Can you see anything?

Tom   Yes. I can see a stomach. But I can't see inside it.

Tim   Would you mind feeling it?

Tom   Do you think you're pregnant? And there was me thinking you were a man.

Tim   I am a man. But I thought maybe you could feel if it was rumbling. That might be a sign of something unpleasant I ate.

Tom feels Tim's stomach.

Tom   No rumbling.

Tim   Nothing?

Tom   You ought to know what you've eaten.

Tim   Macaroni cheese.

Tom   Not exactly heavy narcotics.

Tim   I might've inhaled particles floating around in the air.

Tom   I don't think there's anything wrong with you. Not with your stomach, anyway.

Tim gets up.

Tim   That was no fun. You don't play properly. You just tell me I'm perfectly all right.

Tom   You're terribly sick, but in the head. I've never come across a worse case.

Tim   Doctor, doctor, please make me well again.

Tom For God's sake I'm not a .. not a ...What did you call me. A doctor? Am I a doctor? Am I a doctor?

Tim Now the record's stuck.

Tom Stuck?

Tim Just like the other guy.

Tom You're perfectly all right. Well, your stomach is.

Tim But my head isn't. Jesus Christ! Cure me, please!

Tom So now I'm Jesus, am I? Actually, I'm not. I'm...I'm ....What was I again?

Tim A doctor.

Tom I'm not a...what was it you said? Doctor? Christ! Where do you get it...what am I trying to say...It all...Where do you get it from? All of it?

Tim I get it all from my head, don't I?

Tom And no influence from anyone else?

Tim Well yes. The politician. That's right. He influenced me.

Tom And you are easily influenced.

Tim And I am easily influenced. But so are you!

Tom We're all easily influenced.

Tim Everything was so nice in the beginning. When we first met. I remember us talking about the warm weather and the crops. And you talked about forest fires. That was really nice. Especially all that about forest fires. Yes and about your wife too. How you sometimes can't remember what she's called. I had a good laugh to myself about that.

Tom We're far too easy...I mean easily influenced.

Tim Is that the politician still influencing us?

Tom We can't blame everything on him. Maybe he was influenced by his party.

Tim Shame I can't remember what party it was.

Tom Yes. D'you really think he was a politician?

Tim Yes. That's clear as daylight now. Only a politician would have been able to influence us such a lot.

Tom I'm influenced a lot by my wife. She's a budgerigar.

Tim Is she now!?

Tom   Yes, she's an extra in a cabaret. She plays a budgerigar. Lovely yellow plumage. She gets to sing a bit too.

Tim   I see.

Tom   Yes, she's totally dedicated to a career as an artist.

Tim   How does she influence you then?

Tom   Well, for one thing I've begun to use dental floss. That's her doing.

Tim   Yes, we're all easily influenced.

Tom   We're all easy. I mean easily influenced.

Tim   Do you remember how it all started? You joked about not remembering your wife's name. That was so nice. I get all sentimental just thinking about it.

Tom   I could say it all over again.

Tim   It wouldn't be the same.

Tom   You think not?

Tim   If you were to start repeating things I'd feel really uncomfortable.

Tom   I often repeat things. On the radio. Sometimes the news doesn't change all morning.

Tim   But that's your job. That's different.

Tom   You know, you're the one who's spoiling everything.

Tim   Me!?

Tom   Yes you. You're a moron. I saw that right away. 'Ahoy there' you said. People don't go around saying 'ahoy there' to complete strangers. I should have walked straight off.

Tim   But you didn't.

Tom   I thought I might be able to help you.

Tim   Like Jesus.

Tom   Like a fellow human being. Man to man, as they say.

Tim   We're base creatures.

Tom   How did you work that out?

Tim   We lack integrity. We should be more honest with ourselves. We shouldn't let ourselves be so easily influenced by a politician.

Tom	I don't think he exists. I think it's all a figment of your imagination.
Tim	I can prove he exists.
Tom	How?
Tim	I can call him.
Tom	I see.
Tim	Yep... D'you want me to?
Tom	Yes please, if you can.
Tim	*shouts* Ahoy there. Are you still there?

A Woman enters stage left. She stands at the back - hesitating.

Tim	No, no we're looking for a man. Could we have a man please.

The woman exits and Jim enters.

Tim	There you are.
Jim	Yes. Here I am.
Tim	*to Tom* Who is it?
Tom	I can't place him.

Jim moves forward to the light on the other side of the road.

Tom	Are you the leader of a political party?
Jim	I can't hear you.
Tim	*to Tom* He's got bad hearing. Shout.
Tom	I can't shout. I've got trouble with my vocal chords.
Tim	Shall I shout for you?
Tom	Go on then.
Tim	*shouts* Ahoy there!
Jim	*shouts* Ahoy there!
Tom	*to Tim* Don't say 'Ahoy there', say 'Good morning'. It sounds much better.
Tim	*shouts* Good morning!
Jim	*shouts* Good morning!

> **Tim**   *to Tom*   What shall I ask him?
> **Jim**   *shouts*   Goodbye!

Jim disappears via backstage right.

> **Tom**   He's gone.
> **Tim**   But now you know he exists.
> **Tom**   I think he was a hallucination.
> **Tim**   *shouts*   Come back out!

No result.

> **Tim**   *shouts*   Come back!

No result.

> **Tom**   Yes, yes you can shout all day. It was a hallucination. Or a 'Lucy' as they call them nowadays.
> **Tim**   Lucy?
> **Tom**   Yes. Lucy.

Tim and Tom turn toward the audience.

> **Tim** *and* **Tom** *in chorus*   Lucy!

They look at one another, then turn to the audience again.

> **Tim** *and* **Tom** *in chorus*   Lucy!

Curtain

ACT THREE

Tom is now standing alone at the crossing. The pedestrian signal is still red. He looks around.

Tom   Where are you?

Silence.

Tom   Where are you?

Silence.

Tom   *shouts* Where are you?

Tim and Jim peep in from the other side of the road, stage right.

Jim *and* Tim *in chorus* Here we are!
Tim   But I have to go now.

Tim disappears stage right.

Jim   *shouts* Here we are!
Tom   We?
Jim   What?
Tom   We?
Jim   *looks around* There's only me. Me! I! Here I am.
Tom   I can see that. What is this? A conspiracy?
Jim   A what?
Tom   It is, isn't it? You're ganging up on me?
Jim   *looks around* There's only me.
Tom   The party, I mean. Is he in the party too?
Jim   Which party? We do live in a democracy, you know.
Tom   I don't know which. I thought you would.

Jim	D'you mean me, or him and me?
Tim	You. YOU you. Second person singular you.
Jim	Me? No, I don't know. Should I?
Tom	Yes, if he's right.
Jim	If who's right?
Tom	The other guy. The one who just left.
Jim	Did he say something about a party?
Tom	Yes. He said you were the leader.
Jim	Yes. That's right. Of the Green Party. That must be what you're thinking of. We want a better environment. For the children. Less exhaust fumes.
Tom	Sounds good.
Jim	Would you be interested in joining?
Tom	Are you trying to recruit me?
Jim	Of course not. I was just trying to be friendly to the man on the street. All part of my job as party leader.
Tom	Yes, you can't afford to be unpopular, can you? I think you, YOU you...I think...what was it again? Unpopular. I think you're unpopular. He...
Jim	Who's he?
Tom	The guy who just left. He called you pig-headed.
Jim	Yes, I know. Didn't he call you pig-headed as well?
Tom	No. He liked me. He said I had a pleasant voice.
Jim	You have got a very pleasant voice. That comes across straight away. A bit like Zarah Leander.
Tim	Come on. Don't go over the top.
Jim	Over the top? Me? Never. I wouldn't know where to start. How d'you do it? Could you teach me?
Tom	Say you were invited to someone's house and you remarked that it was like something out of a fairy tale. That would be going over the top.
Jim	What if it really was like something out of a fairy tale?
Tom	It wouldn't be.
Jim	It wouldn't be. I see.

Short silence.

Jim   It's warm out today.

Lights change. They both start to cross the road. They meet in the middle. They shake hands.

Jim   Well hello. My hands are so sweaty. Nervous. Cold sweat. Life's not easy.

Tom   We're standing in the middle of the road.

Jim   Like two digestive biscuits.

Tom   Digestive biscuits?

Jim   Remember? The old schoolboy joke? Two digestive biscuits walking down the road. One gets run over and the other one says...

Tom   Oh crumbs... Yes very good. Meanwhile here we are, in the middle of the road, two cabbages about to be run over and left as vegetables for the rest of our lives.

Jim   *smiles* Yuk! That's awful. Which way do we go then?

Tom   I think I want to go back to my side.

The signal turns red again. They look around.

Tom   What do we do now? It's red.

Jim   No problem. We can cross. Better to walk than stand and talk. Boom-boom! Old Chinese proverb.

They cross to the left side, and stop by the light.

Tom   Well here I am again.

Jim   All present and correct. Well I never! I've been here before.

Tom   You too?

Jim   Yes. This is where I came into the world. Plop! Right here.

Tom   Really?

Jim   Yep. This is where I was born. There used to be a hospital here.

Tom   *points down* Here?

Jim   Around here. They've pulled it down now.

Tom	Really?
Jim	Yep. It's true.
Tom	Well I never.
Jim	Never what?
Tom	What?
Jim	I see. You never what. Interesting.
Tom	Now you've lost me completely.
Jim	You never what? Tell me?
Tom	I never saw my honey honey look so yummy yummy yummy.
Jim	That's not bad.
Tom	A bit amateurish maybe. Reminds me of pop a bit.
Jim	Pop music?
Tom	Yes, exactly.
Jim	The woman I love adores pop music.
Tom	Bravo!
Jim	Why do you say that?
Tom	I don't know. Bravo!
Jim	Thanks anyway.
Tom	Somebody loves you. You're sure, are you?
Jim	Yes, but she loves pop music more than me.
Tim	Sad.
Jim	Worse things happen at sea. Now, how about a drink?
Tim	It's a bit early to start drinking, isn't it?
Jim	I suppose so, but I need to drown my sorrows.
Tom	Are you depressed?
Jim	I feel much better already. All I needed was for you to ask. Makes me go all sentimental. Have you noticed that we seem to be getting on well again now? Don't you think?
Tom	No, I don't. I don't get on with people. Once I was a nice person. I'm not any more.
Jim	Why's that?
Tom	Don't know. Probably because I do all sorts of nasty things.

Tom places his hand on his crotch.

Tom   What d'you think about that, then?

Jim   That's pretty nasty.

Tom   And yet you're looking at a man totally at peace with himself.

Jim   You look like a man on the verge of a nervous breakdown.

Tom   Your fertile imagination, my friend, your fertile imagination.

Jim   I don't understand why we've started being unpleasant to each other. Why don't we both try and be nice.

Tom   All right then, I'll give it a go. 'I like that one. That's a good one. Ha-ha-haa'... Shakes his head. 'Oh yes. That's a good one. Ha-ha-haaaaaaaa!! Too much. Stop it. Stop...HA-HA-HA-HA-HA...Stop it, I can't take any moooore..!'

Tom doubles up with laughter.

Jim   *shakes his head* What the hell's going on?

Tom stops laughing and smiles at Jim.

Tom   I was trying to make myself believe you were funnier than you really are. To cheer myself up. And it worked! I'm in a great mood now.

Jim   You're a funny one.

Tom   No, I'm not. I'm neutral.

Jim   What?

Tom   Neutral. Like Sweden. I'm a radio newsreader, so I have to remain neutral at all times.

Jim   Well you certainly look pretty neutral.

Tom   Thank you.

Jim   What are you thanking me for? It was meant as an insult. Come on man. React! Hit me!

Tom   I thought we were going to be friends.

Jim   I forgot. I forget very easily.

Tom	Perhaps there was a misunderstanding. The fact is I'm neutral. It's not an easy thing to be. It's like being neutered. An 'it'.
Jim	Hm. It. Is that it?
Tom	Yes. That's it. See what I mean?
Jim	I get it. I think.
Tom	Which might lead you to think that I can't have any opinions about anything.
Jim	It might.
Tom	But you'd be wrong. I've got all sorts of opinions. Secret opinions.
Jim	Opinions about what?
Tom	That's secret.
Jim	What's the point of having them then?
Tom	That's secret too.
Jim	Do you feel the same way I do - about the environment - that we have to give top priority to environmental issues?
Tim	I can't say.
Jim	But you said that it sounded good - what I said about reducing exhaust fumes.
Tom	I don't remember that.
Jim	I have a mega-memory. I remember.
Tom	I might've only said it to be polite.
Jim	But who thinks exhaust fumes are good?
Tom	Feel free to draw whatever conclusions you will. My lips are sealed.
Jim	Sealed like a tomb. Like Death. Death doesn't talk either. Dead men speak no ill.
Tom	Luckily for us.
Jim	Maybe. Most people would get angry if someone likened them to Death.
Tom	I haven't got an ounce of aggression in me.
Jim	Rather like Death.
Tom	God! I feel very lonely today. I'm wasting away in my solitude.
Jim	Maybe you need a little company.

Tom	Yes maybe.
Jim	Death in need of company. Best watch my step.
Tom	Is that supposed to be funny?
Jim	Yes. A demonstration of my keen sense of humour.
Tom	A demonstration of your weird sense of humour, more like.
Jim	You're not the first person to tell me my sense of humour is weird. But isn't the whole thing weird? One person says something. Another person laughs. It's weird. The body begins to twitch. Suddenly there seems to be a live eel wriggling in the stomach. Strange noises emanate from the mouth. Hey presto! This thing we call laughter.
Tom	But I'm not laughing, am I?
Jim	Aren't you?
Tom	No, can't you see? Points to his mouth. I'm not laughing. You're not funny.
Jim	You might be laughing secretly.
Tom	I'm crying secretly.
Jim	So am I.
Tom	I see!
Jim	Yes. We're both very depressed.
Tom	Why are you depressed?
Jim	Why are YOU depressed? You go first.
Tom	No, you go first. I asked first.
Jim	No, you go first. I'm older than you.
Tom	No, I'm older than you.
Jim	How old are you, then?
Tom	That's a secret.
Jim	Is that why you're depressed?
Tom	No.
Jim	Must be the environment then... All those exhaust fumes.
Tom	I'm afraid I'm not in a position to comment on that. It might be true, and therefore I am unable to give you a firm answer. As for my being depressed due to my age being a secret: that's so ridiculous that I can reply with a categorical 'no'. But I cannot respond similarly to your subsequent suggestion.

Jim So there is some truth in it, then.

Tom I didn't say that, though my words did carry the implication that there may lie a kernel of truth there somewhere.

Jim Can we stop this now? Let's talk about why we're depressed. I'll go first, then you.

Tom Fire away!

Jim I think it's because I talk too much.

Tom I see.

Jim Yes. When everything goes quiet I get nervous. I think they're after me. I hear footsteps and cars and birds and God knows what.

Tom That's why you talk so much, is it?

Jim Yes. That's my secret.

Tom I talk a lot too.

Jim Good. No risk of uncomfortable silences then. Now tell me why you're depressed.

Tom Because I've got a toothache.

Jim That's no reason to be depressed.

Tom Yes it is. I'm scared of the dentist. For a while I thought you were a dentist and I very nearly ran off.

Jim Some childhood memory haunting you perhaps?

Tom I've never been to the dentist. That's why I get such terrible toothache all the time. It's enough to make anyone depressed.

Jim Come on, I'll go with you.

Tom You're trying to trick me.

Jim Why don't we have them all pulled out. Then you won't have to worry ever again.

Tom What would I to use to eat with, then?

Jim You'd have to suck.

Tom I wish I'd never told you now.

Jim Too late. I'm not going to give up till you go to the dentist.

Tom You're cruel.

Jim At last, someone's said it.

Tom You agree, do you?

Jim   Oh yes. Cruel. Definitely. But no-one's ever had the guts to say it. May I shake you by the hand?

They shake hands.

Jim   Brother, I respect you. You have shown courage.

They let go of each other. The signal turns green again, Tom looks up at the little green man.

Jim   Ignore that. I'm so excited.
Tom   Yes, I'd noticed.
Jim   At last someone's seen the truth. I'm cruel. That's the fact of the matter.
Tom   Someone who's cruel has no reason to look so happy.
Jim   Why not? Does it make me less cruel if I look happy.
Tom   Being cruel is no cause for rejoicing.
Jim   I see. Well I think it is. And I should know better than you, seeing as I'm the one who's cruel!
Tom   I never saw my honey honey look so yummy yummy.
Jim   Yoo Hoo - you're off again...
Tom   I was just trying to stop you thinking about yourself.
Jim   Well it didn't work.
Tom   No, you're off in your own little world, aren't you?
Jim   Nothing but criticism. You must really loathe me.
Tom   You're not worthy of such strong feeling.
Jim   I must be worthy of a little contempt?
Tom   Not even that. I don't even notice you any more.
Jim   I see. *Jim waves at Tom.* You must notice that.
Tom   No.

Jim puts his hand down.

Jim   So I've become invisible, have I?.
Tom   Invisible.

The signal turns red again.

Jim	Yes, I've been trying to perfect that little trick for a while now. I'm quite keen on the old Zennish-Buddhist type of stuff, you know.
Tom	I was speaking metaphorically. If I tell someone I'm not aware of him, I mean he's completely insignificant. Unworthy of my attention. And if you're not worthy of someone's attention, how can you be worthy of his contempt?
Jim	And yet I'm a successful politician.
Tom	Well I don't see how you managed to get yourself elected. I can't imagine many people voting for you.
Jim	I thought you said you never got aggressive. You said you didn't have an ounce of aggression in you. You see. I told you I had a mega-memory. What was all that if it wasn't aggression?
Tom	It was love. We hurt the ones we love.
Jim	So you love me, do you?
Tom	It was a joke.
Jim	I know that. I was playing along.
Tom	We don't crack very good jokes.

Jim and Tom turn to the audience.

Jim *and* **Tom** *in chorus* We don't crack very good jokes.

They turn to face each other again.

Tom	Bad jokes and not getting any better.
Jim	That's why we're depressed.
Tom	No, I'm depressed because of my toothache.
Jim	That was another bad joke.

Tom opens his mouth wide and contorts his face to show his teeth.

Tom   My teeth are no joke.
Jim   *points at Tom and turns to the audience* But he is.

Tom stops.

Tom   You're a nitwit.
Jim   You're just a twit.
Tom   And you're just a nit.
Jim   So we're a nit-twit.
Tom   Yes. Not nitwits. Just one. One nitwit.
Jim   Exactly. What a way to end up. No wonder we're depressed.
Tom   It's my toothache making me depressed.
Jim   But that was a joke, see? Not a very good one, but still a joke.
Tom   My toothache's no joke.
Jim   You mean you really have got toothache?

Tom nods.

Jim   You should go to the dentist then, shouldn't you?
Tom   No, no, no. You're trying to trick me again!
Jim   Are you Death?
Tom   Yes... That was a joke.
Jim   Should I laugh?
Tom   Laugh man!
Jim   I can't laugh. All that aggression's coming back. You're bursting with it.
Tom   It's been building up recently.
Jim   You mean during the last couple of minutes?
Tom   We're all susceptible to change. That's what art's all about.
Jim   Yes. Maybe I could become a dentist.
Tom   Help! What am I going to do?
Jim   Is this another joke?
Tom   I don't know. Suddenly I'm not sure of anything.

Jim	You're not sure who you are? That drastic a change?
Tom	I think so. Who am I?
Jim	Is this a joke?
Tom	I don't know. Is it?
Jim	You ought to know.
Tom	But who am I?
Jim	You're you.
Tom	And you?
Jim	I'm me.
Tom	I see. That explains everything.
Jim	That was a joke. Right?
Tom	I wish I could be struck by a bolt of lightning.
Jim	Why?
Tom	I want to be electric. Then I could give you a shock.
Jim	Give me one of your jokes then. They're shocking! Ha-ha-ha! That was terrible.
Tom	No matter. Everything's terrible.
Jim	I wish I could be struck by a bolt of lightning.
Tom	Why?
Jim	I don't know. Bet you thought I was going to say that I wanted to become electric too, so I could give you a shock, and you could make a crack about my shocking jokes, and tell me how terrible it was. No?
Tom	I can tell you how terrible it was without going through all that rigmarole, thank you very much.
Jim	Call that a joke?
Tom	Call that funny?
Jim	*in an affected voice* Call that funny funny, honey honey?
Tom	*sings* Whimma-wheppa whimma-wheppa whimma-wheppa ooo-io-i-i-oooio ... *As in the song: 'The Lion Sleeps Tonight'.*
Jim	*starts drumming on the floor, front stage* UP THE GREENS!!! UP THE GREENS!!!
Tom	*sings* Ooioo-i-ioo ... The Lion Sleeps Tonight...
Jim	*continues to drum on the floor, front stage.* UP THE GREENS!!!

Tom *sings* Whimma-wheppa whimma-wheppa ooo-io-i-i-ioo...

Jim *drumming* UP THE GREENS!!!

Tom *to Jim* I need to go to the loo.

Jim *drumming* UP THE GREENS!!!

Tom *shouts* I need to go to the loo!

Jim *looks around* Then there'll only be me again.

Tom That's right.

Jim It's still red.

Tom So what. I'm not going to cross anyway. *Tom exits left.*

Jim *pensive, serious* And I need a drink of water. *Jim exits left.*

Curtain

Munich — Athens

A comedy about love

by

Lars Norén

Translated by Gunilla M Anderman

Lars Norén

Characters   Sarah
                    David
                    Guard
                    Woman

Curtain up swiftly on Munich Central Station. Platforms with glass roofs, railway tracks, and in the distance the station building with seven doors and a clock showing the time. It is three minutes past five in the afternoon. We see the end carriages of five different trains and on one of the platforms a sign showing MÜNCHEN — ATHINAI and the departure time: 17:18.

A Woman of about sixty approaches from the far end of the platform, stage front. She is wearing a huge, faded leather coat, which trails along the ground behind her, black slacks, and leather boots. Everything is black except the great mass of white hair. In her hands she is holding a small children's umbrella. It is made of plastic with small Donald Ducks printed all over it. Her lips painted in heavy, black lipstick, she is the very image of evil personified.

Sarah comes running out of the station building, a suitcase in each hand. David follows her at a distance, relaxed and unruffled.

Sudden panic and aggressive flapping from a crowd of pigeons taking off.

Then, gently, from the station loudspeaker float the strains of the Duet from Cosi Fan Tutti. Music at dusk. Tracks and trains glisten in the sultry May air. The atmosphere is charged with sensuality.

Sarah   *suddenly stops and turns round* David! What are you doing? Are you coming, or not?

David   *biting into a very hot bratwurst* Ich komme, my liebling, ich komme. *Smiles.* Coming ... I'm coming.

On seeing David the Woman's face lights up, as if she knows him well. She raises her hand against the black backdrop of the evening sky and scratches at the air. He lifts a hand in reply. She says something but he shakes his head, then stops and puts down his plastic bag. It is all the luggage he has, but his pockets are bulging with bank notes - £1200 spending money for the journey or alternatively, if need be, to cut it short. They have already been travelling for twenty-four hours, having started in Stockholm and passed through Copenhagen and Hamburg on their journey to Athens.

Sarah　Daviiiiiid!!

David continues to talk to the Woman but it is impossible to hear what they are saying.

Sarah　What are you doing?

David laughs uproariously at something the Woman is saying.

Sarah　David, are you coming? *Pause.* Are you? Or I'm leaving.
David　Leaving? Where would you go?
Sarah　Why should I tell you!? I need help. Can't you see!? Why don't you help me?
David　Calm down Sarah. There's plenty of time. It won't leave for a while yet.

Sarah glares at him but he ignores her anger. She opens a door to the train and starts struggling with her suitcases to get them on. She climbs aboard with 'I-wish-I'd-never-set-eyes-on-you' written all over her back.

David　*calls out* What are you getting so worked up about? *To the Woman, intimately and with great intensity.* She's driving me crazy. I don't know what to do with her. She's been carrying on like this ever since we got on the train last night. Five minutes and I wanted to get off. She won't even let me out of the compartment. I've suffered from constipation three times in my life, and each time I'd been in her company for more than twenty-four hours. I'll look a sight when we get down to Athens. *Looks with concern in Sarah's direction.* I have to go. The train's leaving any minute now.

David points to the train. The Woman smiles but continues to talk. Suddenly David looks very serious. She clings to him. He frees himself. She hugs him and starts caressing his chest underneath his shirt. He frees himself forcibly, walks up to the door of the train which has been left open and shouts:

David	Sarah! Sarah! Where on earth are you?
Sarah	*appears, steps down onto the platform* Filthiest train I've seen in my life. Even worse than in Russia.
David	Sarah...
Sarah	No. *Pushes away his hand offering her the bratwurst.*
David	What's wrong? What've I done?
Sarah	If you don't know I'm not going to tell you.
David	No? Why not?
Sarah	And I've got a headache. *Pause.* Athinai? *She looks young and vulnerable.*
David	Yes. That's where we're going. Athens. *Waving goodbye to the Woman.* That's what it's called.
Sarah	Good. At least you know that much. You don't seem to know who you're going with though. Better decide. Her or me?
David	Difficult decision.
Sarah	Yes, I can see that.
David	*puts his arm around her and kisses her on the forehead* Look. Nice isn't it? Look at the pigeons.
Sarah	I'm looking. They're pretty filthy too.
David	Are you hungry?
Sarah	*with distaste* Did you know her?
David	Who? *He has now finished his sausage and is busy licking his fingers clean.* I'd love another one of those... That was my mother.

Sarah	David, please don't. You're getting it all over me!.. Please, David, get on now! Please can't you get on and behave normally just for once?
David	I don't know. Makes me feel strange every time I try.
Sarah	And stop being so manic... But it really is a filthy train, you know. Even the trains in Russia are better than this one.
David	All right. Let's see if we can find a train going to Russia, then.
Sarah	You're always eating. Never stop, do you? Eat, eat, eat. It's very aggressive.
David	Brings out all your aggression, you mean. *Suddenly starts looking at the train more closely.* It'll be all right once we get started.
Sarah	Maybe.... Or all my fear.
David	Nothing to be frightened of, Sarah.

Glimpse of the Guard.

Sarah	And there's no sleeping car. Did you know that?
David	No, I didn't. God, that's going to be fun.
Sarah	No one else seems to be travelling. Only the three of us.
David	Three? Who's the third?
Sarah	You.
David	But why isn't there a sleeping car? *Pause.*
Sarah	How should I know?

Hands in pockets, David saunters gracefully along the platform, the orchestra director, all white tails and silk underwear, before his musicians.

David	What a luxurious feeling, setting off... Have I got time to nip back and get another bratwurst?
Sarah	Why don't you? Go ahead... *Referring to the Woman.* She's mad. *Musing.* Just like everyone else, I suppose.

A Yugoslav Guard comes walking along the platform.

David   Good evening, Sir. Guten Abend, mein Herr. *Points to the train.* Athens 18:18? *No answer.* Athinai? *No answer.* Nein? Beograd, vielleicht? Nicht? Why nicht? *No answer.* Sagen Sie mir, bitte?

The Guard gets on the train. He ignores David, dismissing him without as much as a glance.

David   The strong, silent type. Always wins. Why can't I be more like that?
Sarah   Yes, why can't you?
David   Well, I wouldn't be here with you if I was, would I?
Sarah   Can I have a cigarette please?
David   But Sarah, darling, why are you so nervous? I'm here. I'm with you.

Pause.

Sarah   Think there's a loo on this train?

The Guard gets off the train.

David   *sees the Guard and the Woman together momentarily* Look! Over there! No, don't say anything.

Pause.

David   *looking at the Guard* What about that macho moustache then? *To the Guard.* Al Ahram?... Ist das den?... Dalmatienexpress? Nein? *No answer.* Tauernexpress? Pas de réponse. *Pause.* Qu'est-ce que c'est? *Pause.*
Sarah   Look over there. It's written in big red letters. Can't you read? Have you got the tickets?
David   Why don't you offer him a cigarette?

Sarah He looks like an arrogant type...

Sarah takes out a packet of cigarettes and offers him one. The Guard takes a cigarette from the packet and waits for her to light it for him. She feels ill at ease at this sudden display of intimacy.

Sarah Quite something, isn't he? *Smiles.*
David Sleeping car? Couchette?
Guard Schlaf nein.
David *politely* So du machen diese trip zu und back, through Deutschland, every woche, hier und dier and...über alles? Doesn't understand German, poor bugger.

The Guard looks at him.

David So du ist lobotomised? Das ist...den reason?... Das ist all that Tito did for you? Du machen this trip, zu und back, through Deutschland, every woche, you must lobotomized born be. Nicht, no, nein, non, n'est-ce pas?
Guard Schweden? Gothenburg? Volvo?
David United States.

The Guard shakes his head.

David Bravo. *To Sarah.* Seems to know his geography.

The Guard puts out his cigarette and places it in his pocket. Shaking his head again he walks off along the platform and gets into a different carriage.

Sarah *looking at her watch* It's leaving. Any minute now. No hard feelings?
David *unhappy, hurt* Never mind my feelings. I'll look after mine if you take care of yours.

Sound of whistle as if train is about to leave. As it lurches forward and slowly starts to pick up speed David steps back, waving.

Sarah   David, what are you doing? Can't you see it's leaving? Hurry up! What are you playing at? What are you playing at? DAVID!

David   You go ahead. Don't worry. I'll catch you up.

Sarah   David, what are you doing? DAVID! *Makes as if to jump off. David is walking, perfectly calm, alongside the train.* David, I'm going to jump off! YOU IDIOT! What are you playing at? DON'T LEAVE ME, DAVID!

David   *getting on* Frightened you, didn't I?

Sarah   *goes for him with both fists* Why you're, you're... horrible... horrible... *Brief pause, then she hits him.* Feel my heart...

David puts his hand on her heart, kisses her, strokes her breast. She kisses him back, clinging to him.
Flutter of the pigeons as they fly off and the sounds of the night grow fainter.

Lars Norén

INSIDE THE COMPARTMENT

Two full length seats facing each other, with bunks above them which can be folded down, a couple of grey blankets, a window covered in dirt, a dustbin and a small plastic table.

On the floor cigarette ends, dust, litter, and shards of broken glass.

David	Sarah?
Sarah	Yes, I'm sitting right here.
David	But do you love me? Isn't it that kind of intense love that might turn into hate any minute... and the sooner the better.. for both of us... *Resigned*.
Sarah	Don't start on that one again. You didn't answer me. Is this some sort of game, leaving me all the time?

Pause.

David	And what did I ask you?
Sarah	Don't remember.
David	But you've got many more answers than I've got questions.
Sarah	*matter of fact* Well, we're on our way.
David	*looks up at her* Yes. Great. *Blows her a kiss.*
Sarah	*aside* Why?
David	How's your stomach doing?
Sarah	How long will it take? When do we get to Athens?
David	I know what we can do. We can have an orgy... Twenty-five past eight.
Sarah	Tomorrow morning?
David	No, the day after... Did you get that lens by the way?
Sarah	Forty-eight hours!? Cooped up in here!... What d'you mean? What lens?

David   The wide angle one you lost, remember? Just before we left. You said you'd get a new one. Or did you find it? You know exactly what I mean.

Sarah   Oh yes. I remember. That lens.

David   You did lose it, didn't you?

Sarah   Yes I did. I'd forgotten all about it. I was hoping you had too. *Gets up.* Think we can get anything to eat on this train?

David   Forgotten yes, but not forgiven. *Brief pause.* Only if it's the Ljubljana train.

Sarah   Good, it is. It goes through Ljubljana.

David   Or maybe not. It might be the Jesinice train. That's the one with the buffet car, I think.

Sarah   I see. We're into sadism now, are we? D'you think you could give me a hand with the cases?

David   *sighs* All right. We're staying here then, are we?

Sarah   D'you mind? D'you mind helping me with these suitcases which I've been carting around all day? Could you put them up there for me please? Thank you very much!

David   I'm only too happy to help you with YOUR suitcases. With ALL your suitcases. *He picks them up and puts them on the top bunk.* This must be a record, Sarah. We haven't even reached the outskirts of Munich, and we're already having an argument. Look! Look, come over here.

Sarah   *gets up* Well, what is it? *Goes over to the window. David stands behind her, puts his arms around her.*

David   Sarah I'm sorry. *Hugs and kisses her, then puts his hand between her legs.*

Sarah   What are you doing?

David   Why? Aren't I allowed?

Sarah   *pause* Sure. Go ahead. *Pause.* Let me know when you're finished.

David   *deflated* I think I've finished now. *Tries to kiss her.* Sarah...

Sarah   Please. Not now. Don't you understand David?

David   What? Understand what?

Sarah	I'm still frightened.
David	*pause* I love trains. Have I told you that?
Sarah	D'you remember where you put the toothpaste? I feel like brushing my teeth. *Steps away from him.* Ooh, my bum. It itches. Always does when I've been sitting down for too long. *Gets up and starts pulling down one of her suitcases.*
David	Sarah look! Look at those houses! Just think what God could've done if he'd had the money... Maybe we'll light a candle later on. God I miss you Sarah.
Sarah	*very happy* Really? You do? Why?
David	I don't know.
Sarah	But I'm right here. How can you miss me? *Has now managed to get down her suitcase.* Look at this! What a mess! *Finds toothpaste and toiletry bag.*
David	*to Sarah as she leaves the compartment* I'll be in all evening. Why don't you drop by later if you feel like it?

He pulls down the window, turns on the tape recorder in the open suitcase and sits there in the breeze from the open window, listening to Quincy Jones' Ai no Corrida.

Sarah	*reappears* Ahh, that's much better. *Pause.*
David	*has been fiddling with the camera* As I said: forgotten yes, but forgiven no. The moment we get to Athens I expect to be presented with a new one.
Sarah	I'll do anything if you'll only stop going on about it... I'm not sure I like the way he looked at me.
David	Probably finds you attractive. *Brief pause.* So do I. Sometimes.
Sarah	Yes? You do? *Sits down provocatively, legs wide apart.* That loo's too filthy even to wash your bum in.
David	You know you often say bum when you really mean something else.
Sarah	This time I meant bum.

Throughout their exchange Sarah is acting more and more seductively, while David becomes less and less interested.

David   You're sure? *Looking out of the window, pointedly.* Look! Look at those trains!

Glimpse of the Guard peering into the compartment, having registered Sarah's provocative pose.

David   Fantastic, travelling like this, isn't it? I'm always expecting some mysterious, sinister looking junction to loom up all of a sudden with long winding lines of trembling trains from Moscow, Rome, Bagdhad, Addis Abbaba...

Sarah   *now aware that her sexual invitation has been rejected is busily pulling her skirt down again* Have you got a cigarette? *Takes off her jacket.* I'm freezing.

As David reaches for his jacket to get his cigarettes out, a big bundle of notes falls out of his pocket and lands on the floor. He lights Sarah's cigarette, then puts the money away.

Sarah   Thank you.

Pause.

The Guard slides open the door, then steps inside, holding out his hand.

David   *laughs* What does he want? *Pause.* Why don't you ask him what he wants?

Sarah   I would've thought he'd like to see our tickets.

David   Well, why don't you give them to him then?

Sarah   I haven't got them, have I? I thought you had.

David   And he wants to look at you too, it seems. Maybe he thinks you're a ticket too. *Hands the Guard the tickets.*

Sarah   *smiles* He's quite young.

David   *to the Guard*   What are you doing? Why are you so aggressive? *Raising his voice.* Aren't you ever going to punch those bloody tickets then? What the hell is he doing? *Pause.* By the way, did I tell you what happened to me in Munich?

Sarah   I thought you popped in to see a porn film.

David   No, I did not pop in to see a porn film, I popped over the street to buy an ice cream. And while I was standing there a blind man came walking along, hitting against the wall with his stick and suddenly he hit me across the leg. So I turned around and belted him one. I had no idea he was blind!

Sarah   You didn't?

As the Guard leaves he winks at Sarah.

David   Bugger off, you! *Gets up and walks out into the corridor.* I'll just see what he's doing.

After a short while he returns.

David   Nothing. *Pause.* You know, I think we've got a little bordello here next door. Two pros in there. What an excellent idea... Ah! Must be for the gastarbeiters.

Sarah   What did you say? *Pause.* Can't you think of something to do? *Pause.* Are you ill or something?

David   *sits down opposite her* No, not at all. *Pause.* Why do you ask?

Sarah   Because you look so well.

David   I do? I'm sorry.

Sarah   Ten years younger than yesterday.

David opens his plastic bag which has written on it, in blue letters, 'Museum of Modern Art. Open every day 11-21'. He takes out a shirt

*he has just bought, pulls off the plastic cover round it, examines it,
pulls out the pins and starts unbuttoning it.*

David   Maybe it's you. *Pause.* Maybe you don't see me the way
I am because of the way you are. *Pause.* Only a thought.
No, I feel good, very good.

Sarah   Why? *Pulls down the window, throws her cigarette out.*
Because your mother is dead? Or because you're free of
your daughter for a couple of weeks?

David   Sarah, please, stop it. And don't throw cigarettes out of
the window like that. I hate it.

Sarah   I know.

David   What if a child gets hurt or something? You can't do
without it, can you Sarah? You can't do without it for one
minute. I have to keep on reassuring you, all the time. I'd
love to but I can't. *Cups his hands.* You've so little idea
of who you are, I don't even dare ask 'Is that you,
Sarah?' when I hear you coming because I'm worried
you'll panic and not know the answer. That's how
insecure you are.

Sarah   *pulls up the window again* I certainly won't mind when
my mother goes and that shouldn't be long now, not with
all the fatal illnesses she keeps telling everyone she's
got... It wouldn't be because of us I s'pose, would it?

David   *unconcerned, is spraying himself with his recent
purchase, a bottle of Cerruti toiletry water* What?

Sarah   You feeling happy. It wouldn't have anything to do with
us, would it?

David   Why shouldn't it? *Spraying underneath his arms,
concluding with a friendly spray in her face.* Did I say I
was feeling happy?

Sarah   *gestures defensively* Yes, you did.

David   Did I? Why did I say that, I wonder?

Sarah   I don't know. You're not planning to wear that shirt are
you? You can't.

David   I can't? I bought it only an hour ago.

Sarah   Too tight I'm afraid. *Brief pause*. Look. See for yourself. Doesn't show when you're standing up, that's the problem... What a pity, very nice shirt really... How much did you pay for this toiletry water?

David   Hell. That's the only clean shirt I've got.

Sarah   Wouldn't hurt for you to look at things before you buy them. That's the problem, making a lot of money. Money's like words to you. Doesn't mean anything, any more.

David   I'm paying seventy-two percent of it back in tax. *Pushes the shirt into the dustbin*. No, that's what I am to you. Just words.

Sarah   Don't do that... You might as well give it to the Guard instead.

David   *pause* Why the hell should I do that? Why? Why should I?

Sarah   Do whatever you like. It's your money. And you're paying for this holiday, too, I know. You've reminded me often enough how generous you've been, just in case I forget to fall all over myself with gratitude.

David   Yes, why aren't you?

Sarah   You've paid for everything, the clothes I'm wearing, everything, right down to my panties. *Pause*. But I won't go on wearing French knickers unless you get yourself a new pair of glasses. Or you won't get your money's worth and I'll just get a cold bum. *Pause*.

David   Sarah, what's wrong? Are you all right?

Sarah   No, it's terrible... You know, you've really got serious psychological problems.

David   I have?

Sarah   You're quite clearly someone with serious psychological problems. But what really worries me is your total lack of awareness of how serious they really are.

David   Bit of bad luck that you didn't manage to work that out before you set out on this wonderful holiday in Athens

with me and had to spend forty-eight hours on a train in
my company, wasn't it?

Sarah   Oh, I've known for a long time.

*Pause. Silence is occasionally broken by Sarah muttering something
like 'No, I really don't know how I'll be able to get through the next
fortnight.'*

David   What? What did you say?... I didn't hear.

Sarah   No... It wasn't very important.

David   Sure?

Sarah   It couldn't have been very important if you didn't hear it,
could it?

David   *laughs as if he finds it amusing* Clever, Sarah, very
clever.

Sarah   I can be much cleverer... Try me.

Pause.

David   I know you can. Sarah, why don't you just tell me what
it's all about.

Sarah   *acts innocent* What d'you mean? *Stretches and almost
knocks over his bottle of toiletry water.*

David   You twit, can't you be more careful.

Sarah   Sorry, I didn't see it.

David   So I s'pose it wasn't there then... I'm sorry I shouted.

Sarah   What's happening in the other compartment did you say?
Pause. What did you say was going on in there?

David   I don't remember.

Sarah   A brothel? *Pause.* That's handy. Maybe I'll try and make
a bit of extra money and pay you back... Be nice if we
both had some money, don't you think, then I'd be able
to afford your expensive tastes too... *Puts up a leg,
provocatively, on the seat opposite.* You didn't mind me
interviewing for that job at the Blue Café, did you?

David   Of course not. You would've had a meteoric career. A new star would've been born... What about your act, had you worked that out? What were you going to do? Put a cigarette in your fanny and smoke it? That way you'd get through twice as many cigarettes a day. *Pause*. I'm sorry. *Pause*. Please forgive me. Do you?

Sarah   No.

David   But God always does.

Sarah   That's part of his job.

David   What is it, Sarah? Why are you so nervous?... Does it make you nervous travelling through Europe like this, in the middle of the night, is that it?

Sarah   Not at all. Why should it? *Pause*. I'm much more widely travelled than you are or ever will be.

David   The guard didn't like it, did he? Met contempt with contempt, didn't he?

Sarah   I enjoyed meeting your brother, did I tell you that?

David   Look, look over there, isn't that wonderful? Look at that junction with all those tracks. Like a Mondrian painting... I love travelling, I love being spirited away to strange destinations.

Sarah   Wouldn't it be nice if they could get away and join us in Hydra. I love their little boy, he's gorgeous. *Starts to laugh*. Sometimes it's so obvious it's almost ridiculous. First the little man, then the big man... Where are we?

David   I can't stand the sight of my brother. *Looking at the timetable*. Next stop Salzburg. Eighteen fifty-eight. Another hour, it's only ten to six now... But I like her, she's very nice.

Sarah   Who? Madeleine?

David   She's so... so... Don't you think? I don't know how to put it.

Sarah   I'll help you. How about ... sexless.

David   *feigns horror* Knives are out, are they?... Or are you bleeding? *Pause*. Do I feel something coming my way?

Sarah   No, my way.

David   My brother happens to be exceptionally obnoxious. He's got all the qualities I most detest in a man.

Sarah   In which capacity do you find him most obnoxious? As a man or as a brother?

David   Both... Can't we just sit here without talking for a while? I'd like to relax... Not say anything, just relax...

Sarah   Funny, I don't mind him, it's her, I just don't know what to do with myself when she starts talking. It's even worse when she tries to think... *Pause*. But what's wrong with him? I just can't see why you don't like him?

David   Because he can't talk about anything without giving it a price. Never stops talking about money. All he ever says is 'How much was it?' and 'What did you have to pay?' and 'A bit excessive, isn't it?' *Musing*. Just like you.

Sarah   Wonderful house they've got, don't you think?

David   No.

Sarah   No? Why not?

David   Too solid.

Sarah   Ah, good, we're picking up speed.

David   Sarah, please, can't you, if only for a minute?

Sarah   What?

David   Keep your mouth shut.

Sarah   I'm sorry I never got a chance to meet her. I would've liked to.

David   Who? What d'you mean Sarah?

Sarah   I'm sorry I never got a chance to meet your mother. Would've been nice.

David   Who for? For her or for you? *Pause*. All right, go on talking then. But I'm warning you, Sarah, it's waking me up, soon I'll have enough energy to get up and give you a wallop.

Sarah   Before she died, I mean. *Pause*. Naturally.

David gets up.

Sarah   What are you doing?

Lars Norén

David does not answer.

Sarah Why is it that every time I start talking about myself you
have to get up and go to the loo?

David Had I known you'd be like this I would've travelled on my
own.

Sarah You should've. You know me, don't you? You should do,
we've been together for seven years now.

David Seven? I thought you said nine not so long ago.

Sarah Well, the last couple of years seem twice as long, don't
they? *Pause.* But that's you losing touch with reality, I'm
afraid, if you think it's you having problems with me. It
isn't, you know, it's me having problems with you.

David Oh, is it?

Sarah Can't we stop it and be friends now?

David Of course we can. That would be nice.

Sarah Why don't you come and sit here then? *Pause.*

David sits down next to her.

Sarah That's better. *Pause.* Look, doesn't it look nice? Like that
painting by Ola Billgren... one of his triptychs... the one
with the Citroen in the street... and a group of farm
houses in the middle with big dark roofs... *Moves closer
to him.*

David Is it raining? *Moves away slightly.*

Sarah They must get very heavy when it rains, those thatched
roofs. *Pause.* You know that don't you... doesn't matter
what it's about. Any conversation can be wired with
sexual tension... *Pause.* What are you thinking about?
Pause. Those trousers are far too big for you.

David I know.

Sarah You must've shrunk. Grown smaller. *With great
tenderness.* Smaller and smaller. *Pause.* And smaller.
Makes it much easier for me to love you.

Pause.

David   *laughs as if he senses the tenderness she feels* Ha, ha...
I thought you were going to say something completely
different.

Sarah   Really? What did you think I was going to say?

*Calmly, seemingly uninterested in his answer, she starts taking off her
stockings, then rummages in her bag and finds a bottle of lotion. She
opens it and proceeds to apply the thin white lotion, which comes
gushing out of the bottle, to her feet.*

Sarah   What did you think I was going to say?.. Why don't we
try a bit of bribery? Maybe we could get a more
comfortable compartment if you waved a couple of notes
at him?

David   You know, sometimes I get this funny feeling you'd like
to kill me. Just pick up a knife and start cutting me up
into little pieces.

Sarah   Do you? Really? Why?

David   *laughs again* Don't know. Do you?

Sarah   *laughs happily* Funny you should say that because
sometimes I get this feeling I'd love to get a knife and cut
you up into little pieces.

David   Why don't you? Maybe it'll make you feel better. *Pause.*
Why are you so cruel to me? I lie awake at night, crying
you know... *Pause.* You don't believe me? It's true. *Gets
up.*

David   *slides open the door; the Guard is standing in the
corridor, his back to the compartment* Hullo there, how
are you? *Closes the door again.*

Sarah   I do, I do believe you... I do believe you lie awake at night
crying... *Pause.* I'd lie awake too if I'd been behaving as
abominably as you all day.

David   Did I tell you I went to a press conference for Suzanne
Frankle yesterday afternoon before we left? You know

who she is, don't you? You know she wrote 'Roots of Violence'?

Sarah   Of course. But I'm surprised you do. Why did you go?

David   So you know what it's about?

Sarah   Yes. About you... Who did you go with? Max? I'm getting hungry.

David   *angrily* Max, what d'you mean? Why would I go with Max? *Pause.* Yes, I did... Stop it or I'll... Anyway, we were sitting there, waiting, and then, when she finally came - *Pause* - she had this great black eye. *Starts laughing.* No?

Sarah   No one but you could possibly see anything funny in that.

David   Well, she couldn't, anyway. She couldn't see at all with her left eye.

Sarah   That's it, is it? Is that what you were going to tell me?

David   Would you like to eat now?

Sarah   Yes. What about you? Aren't you hungry?

David   No.

David dives into his big bag again and this time comes out with another, smaller plastic bag, which, it emerges, contains Chinese food - Pacific prawns, sweet and sour sauce and fried rice - which he proceeds to set out on the little table.

Sarah   I don't think I'm very hungry either.

David   Pity we never got to Berlin. There's supposed to be a very good Chinese restaurant there.

Enter the Guard. David pretends he does not see him. The Guard extends a hand, is shown the tickets, examines them, deliberates.

Sarah   *busy eating* Aren't you going to have any?

David   You don't have to gobble it all up, do you? Leave some for me.

Sarah   What is he doing?

David   I don't know. Just as well. Something nasty, I'm sure. Just wait until we get into Yugoslavia sometime in the middle of the night!

Guard   *shakes his head* Stockholm.

David   Yes?

Guard   United States. *Leaves*.

David   *shouts after him* Chicago!

David   *abruptly* All right, let's have it then! *Pause*. What is it? Come on. What is it?

Sarah   Nothing.

David   Come on, let's have it. Tell me or I'm getting off at the next stop. Come on, out with it!

Sarah   I can't think of the right way to put it.

David   Let's have it the wrong way then.

Sarah wipes her hands, throws the empty food boxes into the dustbin, having first rescued the shirt. She opens her bag and pulls out a sheet of paper.

Sarah   So I thought I'd better write a letter instead.

David   *instantly* No. No thank you. No letters. I don't want any letters. *Pause*. No letters. I DO NOT want any letters.

Sarah remains silent.

David   Or if you've written a letter to me please put it in an envelope and post it when we get to Athens and it'll be waiting for me when I get back... But I refuse to sit here being force-fed your profundities. I just won't... If you've got something to say to me why don't you just say it? It's bad, don't you realise, really bad if you feel you can't talk to me, surely you understand that?

Sarah   But I can't talk to you.

David   You'll have to! Try!

Sarah   I've been trying for seven years.

David   I must've had well over six hundred letters from you already. All very sick, all totally incomprehensible. No, thank you. No! Give me the letter, give it to me! *Snatches the letter and throws it out of the window.*

Sarah   Stop it, David, stop it. Stop behaving like that. Like some sort of psychopath!

David   Why? Why can't I? Why can't I if I feel like it? Who's going to stop me? You? Or a letter from you? *Pause.* Please, Sarah... We've just set out on this wonderful holiday together, we're on a train, it has already cost me over three thousand... Must you, Sarah?

Sarah   *very calmly* You're the sickest man in the whole world, the most neurotic person I've ever had the misfortune to meet... God, I can't wait till I get home again! *Pause.* David, why don't you go for a walk? Could you please go for a walk?

David   Why don't you go for a walk?

Pause.

Sarah   I just wanted to put a couple of questions to you, that's all.

David   *pause* Fine, why don't you. Put them over there. *Points.* I'll pick them up later.

Pause.

Sarah   *remains silent* I always seem to end up in places like this when I'm with you. Is it going to continue for the rest of my life, I wonder?

Pause.

David   I hate that black jacket you're wearing. And that black skirt. And those black shoes and those black eyelashes. And that big black cloud hovering over you.

126

Sarah	I always wear my black jacket ... *Pause.* ... because I'm always short of money.
David	Could it possibly be about Max again? Is that what it's all about?
Sarah	Max, what d'you mean?
David	That's why you've been a bit distant lately, is it? So has he. *Pause.* What did you write in that letter?
Sarah	Why don't you run back and get it? Then you can read it.
David	What was it about?
Sarah	I thought you said you weren't interested? *Pause.* I see. So you are interested after all are you?
David	*pause* No. *Smiles.*

Pause. The train pulls to a halt, suddenly.

David	*looking at his watch* We should be in Salzburg any minute now.

David gets up and pulls down the window. Outside it is getting dark and there is rain in the air. We get the feeling we are high up, among green, tree covered mountains.

David	Sarah come here, come and feel the air! Isn't it wonderful!

David is happy. He takes out a bottle of Pernod and pours out two glasses. He pulls her close and hugs her. A blackbird sings in a shivery, throaty voice.

David	*gets the bottle* Here, have some. *Pause.* Get a bit tipsy.
Sarah	Why? *Pause.* No, I'm freezing... I just don't understand, it's all too difficult for me, I'm getting nowhere... It feels as if I'm stuck, as if I can't get out, I never ever feel free, no, it's not only with you...
David	Sarah...
Sarah	Time's up soon and I don't seem to be getting anywhere.

David   Yes, you are, you're getting closer to Salzburg by the minute. Now who was it again who used to live in Salzburg?

Sarah   Mozart.

David   That's right!

Sarah   I'm always nervous, I really am, I'm nervous all the time. Hard to believe isn't it? But it's true. Like I was someone else's lost property, just the way I used to feel when I was a child. As if I can't make a decision because I'm not really allowed to make up my own mind... Like the will to do it and the words to say it are just stifled inside me ... *As if in answer to an unasked question.* ...just die and grow cold, like the children I see in therapy all the time. You understand? Are you listening?

David   I'm listening, I'm listening. Do I have a choice?

Sarah   And I'm drinking too much.

David   Yes you are. Why is that?

Sarah   *close to tears* Because I feel terrible... You see, when we finally get to see the children it's... it's already too late... they don't want any help any more... they're already dead...

David   *quietly* That's awful.

Sarah   Think so?

The blackbird sings again.

Sarah   I feel like that man who was given a new heart. 'I don't want to know anything about the donor', he said.

David   I don't understand.

Sarah   I don't either. *Pause.* I'd love the real Sarah to step forward. I've been waiting for her for so long... I want to find out what she wants to do, doesn't matter if it isn't much and just do it... And if I decide to let someone into my life they won't rule it or take it over ever again... I'll be a small planet in a dark void... That's what I dreamt last night... a little planet that was attached to a big

128

planet, both glowing white in a black void and suddenly the little planet freed herself and left a great big hole in the big planet... And the little planet said to the big planet... don't cry, maybe I'll come back, from time to time, but only on my terms... When I see someone who's happy I start crying... When I see joy and happiness... people doing what they like doing so much that they forget about themselves... I do feel happy too, sometimes... but the only way I can express it is crying... that's my happiness... My feelings are so strong they're no longer emotions ... *Aggressively.* I can't do what I want to do. I can't because I don't have a self. Because it's not my own any more, it's yours.

Pause.

Can you hear? ... They're swallows... Did you know that pilots have seen swallows three thousand metres above ground?... Do you know what they do up there?... They sleep... And still, it's really quite simple. I won't die if you don't love me any more... I do understand it all... I know the facts. If I moved in with you it'd be much more difficult if we split up... I know, I do understand that it'd be difficult... I do realize what it'd be like for me... but I still refuse to accept the logic of it... I'm up there, flying, soaring above it all, I still think I can do it... I won't die if we stop seeing each other... It isn't that I need looking after, I can take care of myself, too well, maybe... Once you were everything... Once I was nothing if I wasn't what you wanted me to be... D'you understand?

David   You're just like a child, talking and talking for hours on end, never tiring.

Sarah   I'm frightened.

David   Me too.

Sarah   But this is about you.

David   No, about you.

The train lurches, suddenly, then starts moving.

Sarah Who wants to be a big fat flop like you anyway? I certainly don't. *Pulls up the window, turns around.* How on earth could you ever write a novel and call it 'The Escape That Never Was'?

David *sits down* I never intended to write a novel.

Sarah Why did you write it then?

David It was long before I met you. Do we have to talk about it?

Sarah *laughs, heartily* You're right, absolutely right, we shouldn't. Nothing to talk about! Ha, ha, ha!

David You know, when you're being vicious I never know if you really are or if you're just making out you are.

Sarah *still laughing* No, I don't know either.

David *starts laughing too* No, I don't either... *Tries to cover up his hurt, fails.* I never know if... you're intentionally unaware of your intentions... *Stops laughing.* How about that? Not bad, eh?

Sarah *very serious* Have you given any further thought to what we were talking about?

David Lucky for you I don't or you'd be in big trouble! *Laughs again, but this time a slightly hysterical note has crept into his voice.* Talking about what? What d'you mean? What were we talking about? We never seem to stop talking... What are you looking at?

Sarah *soberly* You know I'm sure there's a lot of dirt that's collected up there, under those ledges...

David Maybe that's where it all goes. All the rubbish we talk.

Sarah David, where do you get it all from?

David You.

They kiss, she audibly, using her tongue, her mouth open.

David What was I supposed to have given some thought to? ... No, stop it, Sarah, stop it, you know how much I like it. Stop it now, please.

Sarah	The discussion we were going to have. You and I were going to sit down and talk about when we're going to settle in together, when we're going to put our dirty laundry together and buy ourselves a washing machine.
David	Oh, that. I haven't had the time.
Sarah	Will you ever?
David	In my next life, maybe. Then we'll talk about it, I promise.
Sarah	*pulls away* Well, I want to know. As soon as possible.
David	You will, don't worry.
Sarah	As soon as possible. When?
David	I told you, didn't I?
Sarah	Yes, but when? ...
David	Soon...
Sarah	But as soon as possible. And preferably before we get back home again so I can start thinking about how I'm going to organize things... if we're going to go on seeing each other or not...
David	What d'you mean 'if we're going to go on seeing each other or not'? What's that supposed to mean?
Sarah	Because if we don't move in together soon... then I'm not sure there's much point in us seeing each other any more.

The train stops, they have arrived in Salzburg. On the platform outside the train window there are vendors, selling newspapers and sandwiches.

David	Sarah, what's wrong? Why are you carrying on like this?

Pause.

Sarah	I'm not, I just don't want to go on like this any more. *Threatening note in her voice.* Don't you understand, I want to live with someone...

131

While she is talking David gets up, slides open the door and walks into the corridor outside the compartment.

	... and be with someone and belong to someone and fall asleep with someone and wake up in the morning with someone. *Very calmly.* I want to be close to someone, I want much more consideration, much more commitment... I'm NOT asking you to - Where are you going?
David	I'm going out to buy a Frankfurter Allgemeine. Like something to drink?
Sarah	Don't go! Please don't go!
David	Oh yes, I will.
Sarah	Don't, please don't go, stay here, please! Every time you leave I never know if I'll ever see you again.
David	Exactly.

David leaves. Almost immediately Sarah runs up to the window and starts looking for him, anxiously, but he soon returns with a couple of newspapers and some sandwiches which he hands to her through the open window while he remains on the platform.

David	What are you NOT asking me?
Sarah	I'm NOT asking you to make some sort of promise that you'll move in with me... although you've been saying that you would for years now but I AM asking you to decide whether you'd actually like to or whether you're just so infantile and immature that... I want to know where I stand... But, of course I don't mind, I can wait till we get to Athens... But then I want a decision.
David	Forget it then.
Sarah	What? What did you say?
David	You heard me. Just forget about it.
Sarah	What d'you mean?
David	You really think that sort of blackmail's going to work?

Sarah	And what about us? D'you really think it's ever going to work if you don't stop being ambivalent?
David	Let's forget about it then, darling. See? That's how ambivalent I am.
Sarah	What d'you mean? You really mean that? David, please get on now!
David	Try me.
Sarah	Why did you say that?
David	I can't be much more ambivalent than that can I?
Sarah	Than what?
David	All right. Forget about it.
Sarah	What? What? Forget about what?
David	The whole bloody thing. You and me.
Sarah	What?
David	Forget about it. Just forget about it.
Sarah	What d'you mean?
David	Forget about it... Us. You and me.

Sarah sits up abruptly, throws her things together in a flying hurry and makes as if she is about to jump off the train. David rushes into the compartment, grabs hold of her and stops her. She starts screaming and hitting him but he holds her, firmly, until the train starts moving again.

David	Sit down! Sit down! Don't ever do that again, d'you hear? Do you hear? *Long pause. Lets go of her.* Sarah, what d'you want? Sit down! Sit down and tell me what it is you want! D'you know what you want? If you do, please tell me Sarah!
Sarah	*sits down* You know what I want. You know exactly what I want!
David	*more calmly* That's what I want too. I can think of nothing I'd rather than you and me settling down together but ... *Searches for words.* ...we've got to go about it the right way. We've got to find a solution to the practical problems, you know that... Where's the money

going to come from, are you going to ask me every morning for enough to see you through the rest of the day? How can we start off like that? We deserve something better, don't we? At least I think I do. We've got to ask more from ourselves, Sarah.

Sarah You're so good at talking about what you should ask from yourself, aren't you? Why is it that you're so bad at doing it when it's asked of you?

David We'll have to see a lawyer and get him to do all the paper work, you know exactly what I mean, all the money I make and all the money you owe and work out some sort of arrangement so I won't find that one day you're living in the flat I paid for and I'm not... And not one single syllable will go down on paper without long drawn out negotiations with me. I'm going to want my pound of flesh and every little drop of blood I can squeeze out of you. *Brief pause.* It's got to be give and take: you give and I take.

Sarah You really want to marry me? You really want us to live together? You and you?

David And you, you mean?

Sarah Yes. You really want to?

David Oh, yes. No doubt about it. Definitely. *Gets up.*

Sarah Why?

David What the hell, stop asking me when I'm - *almost trips -* when I'm wearing these bloody shoes, will you!

Glimpse of the Guard.

Sarah He's got nice eyes... Not my type though. You are. You're my type.

It is now quite dark and David starts looking for the lights. Having finally found them he switches them on, two tiny little lamps. It is now well past eight o'clock in the evening.

Sarah   I'm just going out for a pee.

While she is away the train stops again. David pulls down the window, lights a cigarette and stands there smoking, at peace with himself. Suddenly there is a sound from outside, first faint, then quite close as if we are hearing something without being fully aware of it. It is a man shouting, in German perhaps, with increasing intensity and then, finally, with full force, uninhibitedly spewing out abuse. Sarah returns. She has put on make-up, silvery glitter which looks like little frozen tears with a bigger, sharp edged tear hanging down from the side of her nose. Outside a Woman screams as if she is being beaten.

Sarah   Where's that? Outside? Can't you hear? *Walks over to the window.* What's going on? *Another scream.* I can't see anything. *More screams.* How awful... Can't you hear? *Pulls up the window but the screaming continues just as loudly.* That's terrible... What are we going to do?

David   I was on my own one night, it was last summer, a very hot and humid night, everybody had their windows open, and I heard this couple making love. It was very quiet and every sound echoed through the night. *While he is talking the train starts moving again.* I heard her breathe, deeply and then more and more quickly, and then I heard her scream, four, five wonderful little screams and they seemed to bounce across to my window and then they rolled, slowly, trembling into my room... I thought it was you for a moment. *Pause.* I like to be there without anyone knowing I'm there and then, when the picture's been developed, you can see I'm there too... Thomas Tranströmer has written something about it, about a fishing boat, out at sea in the early morning mist. 'The six men on board didn't know we were seven'... I remember an interview I did with a painter once and there was a photographer there as well to take photographs. And the painter turned to the photographer and said 'Go on, take your pictures but it'd be much better if I don't know.

	Much more natural that way.' And then he got up and just walked out of the room.
Sarah	But... but David... I just want you to marry me and show the world you belong to me... So they'll leave me alone, but I s'pose that was not to be... *Reaches for the bottle.*
David	Should you? Should you really drink any more?
Sarah	Yes, of course I should. Why not, why shouldn't I, I'm on holiday, aren't I? *Pause.* I thought you liked it when I get a bit tipsy... *Suddenly, in a sensuous voice.* You love it, you know you do, my little porcupine, when I get all soused and sexy... and - *Covers her face with her hand, starts licking the inside of the palm and her fingers* — ... and gone and gooey... wow... *Her tongue starts darting back and forth* ... your very own, squiffy little waitress. And as she bends over and tries to pick up her tip from the floor - *gives a shudder* - all those fishy eyed and frothy mouthed old fogeys try to plant a kiss on her bum.
David	All right, very good, go on... You know I hate it.
Sarah	*with indifference* Do you? Good.

Pause. But nothing happens.

Sarah	*quite different, now very lucid* This feeling of unbounded happiness that you can get - me too, sometimes - that's nothing but the sand cascading when you first start running. Only the beginning of the race...
David	I like that... The sand cascading... Is that what you said?
Sarah	Yes.
David	Nice... And we are the runners are we?

Suddenly he falls asleep. Sarah picks up his newspaper and starts reading. Pause.

David	*wakes up* Eh?
Sarah	You were asleep.
David	How did I look?

Sarah	I don't know. Like you were asleep.
David	Has anyone been here?
Sarah	No. Why?
David	Where are we? What time is it? *Looks at his watch.* It's late, almost one! We should be in Villach any minute now.
Sarah	Where's that?
David	Austria, I think.
Sarah	Austria? I didn't know we were travelling through Austria.
David	Umm... Why don't we go to bed now.
Sarah	I'm too tired.
David	Here he comes again. What does he want this time?

The Guard enters, wants to see the tickets.

David	What the hell is going on? How many times are you going to look at them?

The Guard does not answer.

David	Get stuffed, will you!?
Sarah	What's wrong? No harm in him standing there if that's what he wants. Why don't you leave him alone?
David	Why, why should I? Tell him, you tell him. Tell him to get lost.
Sarah	He's just being a bit childish, that's all. Nothing to get worked up about.
David	No, I've had enough. Piss off! Out!
Guard	Tickets!
David	No, you can't see them. Bugger off!
Guard	Sit down you git and shut up!
David	What? What was that? What did he say??

The Guard turns to Sarah and starts talking to her in Serbo-Croat. She answers him, in Serbo-Croat too, and they start conversing.

David   What are you talking about?

Sarah laughs.

David   Stop that.

Sarah   I'm only asking him what his name is and where he lives...

David   Why? Why are you asking him that? Listen Sarah, enough! Make up your mind. Who are you travelling with? Him or me? ... *To the Guard.* Can't you hear!! Piss off I said!! Leave us alone! *To Sarah.* Tell him Sarah, tell him. Ask him to leave, please!

Sarah says something in Serbo-Croat and the Guard leaves.

David   Why did you do that?

Sarah   What? Do what?

David   You know what I mean.

Sarah   I didn't do anything... You mean I can't even talk to another man? You feel threatened that easily?

David   What were you talking about?

Sarah   Oh, nothing, just talking.

David   You wait... Just you wait.

Sarah   I will... How long d'you think I'll have to wait?

David   Just you wait... Twelve more days.

Sarah   Just you wait... Twelve more minutes.

David   What the hell d'you mean by that? *Pause.* Stop it, Sarah, or I'll get off... Just you wait... *Looks at his timetable.* ... at... at Rosenbach... I mean it, Sarah, really.

Sarah   Yes, you do that.

David   What? What d'you mean?

Sarah   You do that. Please do that, please get off the train. Let's split up again. Let's split up in... in Rosenbach or whatever it's called.

David   All right then.

Sarah   Good.

David   You'd better be careful!

Sarah   I will. You too.

David   YOU get off. *Pause*. Sarah, why are you carrying on like this?

Sarah   I'm terribly sorry. I had no idea you'd feel threatened just because I exchanged a couple of words with another man. I promise I won't do it again. Never ever. I won't talk to anyone. I won't open my mouth until we get back home again. And then I'll only talk to my mother. Is that all right? No one else, just my mother.

David   You can talk to whoever you like. Do whatever you like. Who cares? I don't.

Sarah   No, no. I'll do whatever you like.

David   No, no. Be yourself. As you always are. A neurotic slut.

Long pause.

David   I'm sorry. *Pause; offers her some wine.* Like some more? *Pause*. What are you thinking?

Sarah   I'm tired.

David   That's all? That's all you're thinking? Just 'I'm tired, I'm tired, I'm tired'? You must be thinking 'I hate you, I hate you, I hate you' as well, aren't you?

Sarah   *does not seem to hear* Since you're offering. Yes, please, I'd like some more.

David   Must you?

Sarah   Ugh, you're so mean it drives me crazy.

David   You're so crazy I have to be mean.

Sarah   And you're so crazy it makes me thirsty... Are you seriously trying to suggest that I can't have another, tiny glass of Pernod? Then, I'm afraid I shall have to go somewhere else.

David   Where? Where would you go?

Sarah   Anywhere... You think I've got no one else to turn to, don't you?... Don't worry, I can manage, much, much better without you... What a relief to get out of your

139

Lars Norén

crazy world which you choose to believe is normal. What a relief!... Or maybe that's just what you want? A relief for you too if you got rid of me? Oh, no, I'm not going to give you that satisfaction, oh no, don't get any false hopes on that score! You're responsible for me, you are, you made me come on this horrible trip with you, I knew I wasn't going to enjoy it... And stop going on at me. STOP IT! *He tries to say something.* SHUT UP! I've known you for seven years now and do you know how I've survived? I'll tell you. I've followed a golden rule, that's how. Every time you go for me I tell myself that it hurts you much more than it hurts me... Yes, go on, you laugh... Who d'you think you are? All I need to do is this - *snaps her fingers* - and I'll have you put away... Even a Yugoslav guard could see straight away that you're completely mad and asked if I was your nurse... You're right, I have been a bit distant lately, I'm surprised you've noticed. You know why? I'll tell you, I'll tell you why. Last Tuesday I broke up with somebody, a man I've been seeing for the last three months and that's why I'm feeling a bit low, not surprisingly... I'm terribly sorry, I'll try and pay closer attention, I'll try...

David Why don't you try something else?
Sarah What d'you mean?
David Try and find your dictionary.
Sarah What?
David I thought you packed a dictionary.
Sarah Why?
David I'd like you to look up the word 'tedious'.
Sarah What d'you mean? I don't understand.
David No, I know you don't.
Sarah Do you love me?
David You?
Sarah Yes... Me.
David Yes. I think so.

Sarah But I don't think so. I don't think you're able to love. Only to run away from it... ... You're very cruel. *Deeply distressed, with real tears in her eyes, almost.* You're foul, you are. Why? Why are you?

David Why? Why am I? The cross I have to bear I s'pose. It's hard work being foul. Why don't we try and get some sleep. Let's see if we can make these beds.

Sarah *as if talking about a common cold* You know it feels as if I'm about to go mad.

David Funny. That's exactly the way I feel too.

Sarah I don't even want to touch these blankets.

David Seem to be army blankets. Maybe we can open a window and shake them a bit.

Sarah Well, if I do, I do, I s'pose. As long as you don't leave me.

David *trying to get the beds ready* What? Of course I won't.

Sarah As long as you don't stop loving me.

The Guard enters and as before just stands there without saying a word although this time he appears to be slightly inebriated. Tension starts mounting. Suddenly David turns to face him, pretends to be startled and jumps with surprise. When the Guard finally extends his hand for the tickets David grabs it and starts shaking it vigorously. The Guard frees his hand forcibly and pushes David so he falls back, onto the seat.

David Hey, you, you watch out! What d'you think you're doing!?

Sarah Better be careful. He looks pretty fierce.

David So do I.

Sarah No, you don't.

David But I am. Very fierce.

The Guard smirks.

David Does it have to look like this? *Points to the cigarette ends on the floor.* Look. And it smells too. Awful. What is this? Yugoslavia?

Sarah   Calm down, David.

David   Tell him, Sarah, tell him. Tell him to leave or we will.

The Guard remains silent. Sarah hands him the tickets. He looks at them, smiles at her and then leaves.

David   He's creepy. *Pause.* I'm going to kill him. *Pause.* I wish we could lock this door. *Pause.* You know, when I think about it, the only time you're ever nice to me is when you're having an affair with somebody else... But we've been together now for seven years, remember, and I can sense it when you're up to something. I know exactly where you are and what you're doing and don't forget, that's what I might be doing too. See, not quite as simple as you first thought eh?

Sarah   What? What d'you mean?

David   Nothing. Why don't you give me a hand? Help me put this on, please. *Pause.* God help him if he comes back again... I feel funny, I don't think I'll be able to sleep.

Sarah   What d'you mean? Once and only once before in my whole life have I been seriously involved with another man and that was with someone I'd been keeping up a correspondence with and I didn't even like him when I finally got to meet him. And only ... *Choking, close to tears.* ... only because I desperately needed some love and affection to be able to ... to FEEL... to feel that I wasn't just being pushed around and laughed at all the time.

David   Forget it.

Sarah   And it was over almost before it started. *Almost hysterically.* And that, that was all... That was all because I knew that if it went on any longer I might lose you. But it didn't change the way I felt about you, if anything I loved you more, not less! If you think you've got any cause to feel threatened or cuckolded or anything else you just don't know how wrong you are!

David   I don't. I'm disconsolate!

Sarah   And please don't turn it into a joke like everything else! I'm serious.

David   My joke was too, very serious... Look, forget it. It didn't mean anything. I can't even remember what I said now. A nasty conditioned reflex, that's all. *Pause.* Get undressed now and dry those self-indulgent tears.

Sarah   It strengthened our relationship, don't you think?... No, I'm not getting undressed... We got much closer, didn't we? You said so yourself.

David   I'm going to sleep.

Sarah   Every time I open my mouth to talk to someone else you get beside yourself, that's how frightened you get... I can't even say 'good evening' to the guard on a train... In fact I can't say anything to anyone any more, can I, without triggering off a stream of vicious witticisms from you? Whatever I say you'll always have the last word, always put the poison in. You'll kill everything, yourself too, in the end.

David   I know... Why don't you bring yourself and your glass of Pernod to bed now?

Sarah   No, I feel as if I've lost interest in everything.

David   Could you give me my bag, please.

Sarah hands it to him.

David   *looks for a mirror, finds it* Good thing you didn't break the mirror. *Opens his mouth and looks at his throat in the mirror.*

Sarah   Why? Would've spared your ego a nasty shock wouldn't it? *Watches as he drinks from the Pernod bottle.* You're sure you should drink any more?

David   No. Nor should you. We're not real men, you and I.

Sarah   I can drink as much as any man. *Pause.* Can't we be friends again before it's too late?

David   It's never too late... Is that what you heard in my voice?

Sarah   Yes. *Pause.* Why are we carrying on like this? I... I feel terrible... I can't bear it when you call me a neurotic slut...

David   No? You know, you're not supposed to take every nasty thing I say personally.

Sarah   I might be a slut in your eyes and if I am it's only because of you anyway, but I AM MOST CERTAINLY NOT NEUROTIC, not as yet anyway, but I probably will be very soon if you continue the way you're going. *Pause.* Neurotic slut... *Pause.* Maybe, why not, sounds rather nice. *Sexually provocative.*

David   I'm very tired, Sarah.

Sarah   If I'd wanted to sit up and listen to someone feeling very tired I might as well have stayed at home with my mother.

David   *looks out of the window, smiles as if something has made him unhappy* Peasants walking home after a day in the field... there's a lesson there for you, Sarah.

Sarah   What is that?

David   They know when it's time to stop. *Pause.* Beautiful, those bulls resting in the shadow of those big trees. Or ... *Puts on his glasses, pause.* ...maybe it's their wives. Come to bed now.

Sarah   You're in bed already?

Pause.

David   Get undressed now, no, don't, just come to bed.

Sarah gets undressed.

David   What's wrong?

Sarah   The bottle.

David   Don't drink any more. *Hugs and kisses her.* So that's what you'd like, is it, Sarah? You'd like us to get married would you? *Drinks.* Well, why not? Let's try it. *Pause.*

We'll get married in Athens. With you barefoot. No, dressed like the first time I saw you, coming out of Café Opera in those little bootees and a white gardenia in your hair... Or maybe they were ballet shoes.

Sarah	A gardenia? A white gardenia? Is that what you want? *Pause.* They were ballet shoes.
David	Yes, I remember. Cream coloured.
Sarah	No, dusty pink. *Pause.* Are we going to make love, is that what you had in mind?
David	Up to you. *Pause.* But you'll wear the clothes you had on the first time we met, won't you?
Sarah	No... What happened outside Café Opera?
David	You walked past, I saw you and my heart stopped.
Sarah	I'm freezing.
David	You don't feel like making love, is that what you mean?
Sarah	No. I'm not saying that. I don't know. Do you? Do you feel like it?
David	I always feel like making love to you.
Sarah	Always?
David	We don't have to.
Sarah	I'd like to in principle, if only it didn't take so much energy.
David	All right, you can have it. You can have the wedding you never had... May I? *Reaches for her glass.*
Sarah	I thought you'd say that. You usually do at this point. *Kisses him.* Ouch -
David	What's wrong? Are you uncomfortable like that?
Sarah	Can't you move a bit? You're not leaving much space for me.
David	You're getting a bit tipsy, aren't you? That's when I usually turn sober.
Sarah	It's nice, isn't it?
David	What is?
Sarah	Just lying here... And getting a bit tipsy.
David	Can you see the stars?
Sarah	No.

David Can you see the guard?

Sarah No, why, can you? Wonder where we are...

David *looking at his watch* Half past twelve already. We must be getting very close to Ljubljana. That means we're in Yugoslavia. *Pause.* By the way, there's something I've been meaning to ask you... quite important, too, but I keep forgetting... What was it now, I'm trying to remember... If only I could... On, yes. Let's see now, let's see if I can get it right... If it's possible ever to get it right... I hope you won't take this the wrong way now, Sarah but... Do you love me? It might be important I think... Do you, Sarah, do you? Do you love me?

Sarah *with great tenderness* But darling, do you really have to ask me if I love you?

David *drily* Who do you suggest I ask then?

Sarah What about you?

David I love you if that's what you'd like me to call it.

Sarah Of course I do. More than anything else in the world.

David I'll love you... forever and ever. But no longer than that...

Sarah And I'll love you... not forever and ever. Much, much longer... *Pause.* Darling, I'm so happy.

David You are? Sure you are?

Sarah Yes... Are you?

David I think so.

Sarah Come on, you must be.

David You are? You really are? You're really feeling very, very happy?

Sarah Yes. As happy as I'll ever be.

David And very, very sexy?

Sarah Well... More like making love than just having sex. Much more... fulfilling, don't you think?

David Yes. But not as much fun. Why won't you let me keep my hand there?

Sarah I thought that's where you usually keep it... You sounded just like a child then.

David But I like it.

Sarah	Yes. When you're hungry or thirsty or unhappy and want your mummy, that's where you go.
David	Wrong!
Sarah	When God was doling out sex, you must've asked for an extra portion.
David	*referring to the Pernod* Doesn't taste that good when it isn't chilled. But I'm persevering.
Sarah	What's it about mine you like so much anyway? What's so special about it? Like everybody else's isn't it?
David	I'm not so sure I should answer that.
Sarah	But it is nice, isn't it? I think so anyway.
David	Yes. *Pause.* So do I. Very, very nice.
Sarah	It'll have to last us for the rest of our lives.
David	It'll do us... But I shall have to find some way of losing twenty pounds.
Sarah	Tried eating less?
David	I will. When we get to Athens. As soon as I have, we'll get married.
Sarah	But tell me, is it? Is it peculiar in any way?
David	Only the colour. Green is rather unusual.
Sarah	Any other colour you'd rather? Black, orange, pink? No, I'm not a punk. But I could be I s'pose. What did you think about that dress she was wearing?
David	Who? Madeleine, you mean?
Sarah	With that slit right up to her navel... Maybe I should get something like that, what d'you think? Do my Saturday morning shopping dressed like that... Can't you do something with your legs?
David	Like what?
Sarah	Like fold them up and put them on the rack or something... Everything's coming off. Where's my other earring gone?... You know I honestly don't think I've ever met anyone as sexless as that prune-faced wife of your brother's. Not an ounce of sex in her whole body.
David	If you're trying to turn me off, Sarah, you're succeeding admirably...

Sarah Or if there is, it's the sort that need to be washed with care every evening, doesn't need ironing and doesn't wrinkle, one hundred percent artificial fibre. And I bet she hangs it up to dry with little plastic clothes pegs.

David Congratulations, Sarah, a magnificent job you did there. I now feel old, ailing and decrepit. Why don't you write it all down. You might be able to use it again, some other time.

Sarah *with vehemence* There won't be enough space for all of us if they come too! We can't all sit in one settee can we?

David It'll be us or them. They can have it. *Pause*. Or he might need all of it, Johnny's so fat he needs a whole settee to himself.

Sarah That's not very nice, talking about your brother like that.

David You're right. Sorry, I didn't mean it that way. What I was really trying to say was: Johnny's so fat he needs a whole settee to himself.

Sarah Maybe we can buy some plastic chairs in Athens.

David Sarah, my darling, d'you realize that I rented this house in Athens to put as much distance as possible between my brother and me? So what do you do? Before we leave you make absolutely sure that you've set a date for them to come and stay with us. *Pause*. It's dark, isn't it. Two o'clock.

Pause.

Sarah What ARE you doing?

David Like it?

Sarah No... It's not happening. Pity, I would've liked to.

David I still do.

Sarah Not in the mood. That matters doesn't it? Or perhaps you'd rather we forgot about that? Forgot about feelings altogether? Don't need them, do we?

David That's right. No need. Not right now, anyway.

Sarah   There is. Right now.
David   Not what I need.
Sarah   No, I know what you need.

Sarah gets up.

David   What's wrong, Sarah.
Sarah   I have to go to the loo.
David   Come on then. The sooner you go, the quicker you'll come back.

He drops the bottle which falls to the floor and breaks.

Sarah gets down, slides open the door and walks out into the corridor, barefoot and wearing only her panties. David steps down, carefully and starts looking for his cigarettes. He finds them and lights one. The train grinds to a halt, slowly, then stops.

On the horizon the lights from a big city.

Suddenly another train pulls up, then stops. It is a French train. David can see straight into another, brightly lit and luxurious looking compartment where two men are kissing. He hears the sound of their voices. A couple of minutes pass, then the other train starts moving again.

Sarah   What's the smell? Ugh! Why don't you close the window? *Pause.* What's wrong? *Pause.* Upset again?
David   What took you so long? What were you doing?
Sarah   What d'you mean 'What was I doing'? What are you getting at?
David   Nothing.

They sit down, she takes a puff on his cigarette, his shirt is hanging loose around his waist. She is wearing his jacket.

David   I wish there was a light inside me I could just switch off.
          Pause. Why? Why do I want to do that?
Sarah   So you won't be able to see what's happening.
David   Think so?
Sarah   I know so.
David   I see.

Pause.

Sarah   *drops ashes on him* Sorry I didn't mean to. Or did I?
David   Good. Love's gone. Now we can start being really nasty
          to each other.
Sarah   That's the way you feel?
David   No, not at all.
Sarah   The end. Love's no more. Nothing to be scared of.
David   But I am. Scared stiff. Terrified.
Sarah   Did I burn you?
David   Doesn't matter, Sarah.
Sarah   That's the way you feel?

The train stops. They have arrived in Zagreb. Outside on the platform there are strange looking men with shaven heads and jerky movements, not unlike the recreation room in a big psychiatric ward. Silently they press their faces against the windows of the train.

David   Where are we?
Sarah   What time is it? If it's a quarter to three we're in Zagreb.

Pause.

David   All right then, let's try it for a year. How's that? Let's
          move in together and see what happens... But don't sell
          your flat, keep it and let it out to someone instead... And
          then you move in with me for a year. A year at a time.
          Each day as it comes. Each hour...
Sarah   Why?

David   Because...

Sarah   No more metaphysical explanations, please. But if you think that I'm just some juicy little melon you can squeeze whenever the mood takes you...

David   I'm sorry?

Sarah   I can't get through to you, can I... You're just like a Jehovah's witness... Won't leave, just stands there... What's the gospel according to St. David then?

David   Nothing, my darling, nothing. I've told you already. A year. A year at a time. Agreed?

Sarah   I'll agree to anything. *Pause.* I've been told you need to be treated with care. This can't be Zagreb, must be a mental asylum.

David   And you won't go off and look for a bridge to jump from if we fail?

Sarah   If you fail, you mean?

David   Since I'm your whole life.

Sarah   I promise. *Pause.* Why would I want to do that? I told you, I'm still trying to figure out what it's all about.

David   I wish I didn't have to wear shoes. I'd much rather walk around in the sorts of sandals they're wearing.

Sarah   They're not sandals, just something made of cloth. I think they must dye their hair with henna.

David   This is where the Orient starts... I think I read somewhere that in the Middle Ages -

Sarah   I can't wait for us to get together properly... Yum, doesn't that look good.

David   Just wait till we get closer to Athens. When you open the window and smell the warm, balmy air... wild thyme, rosemary, oregano... I think we're leaving.

The train starts moving. Some of the men follow, running along side the train as it pulls out.

David   Want to know a secret?

Sarah   Yes. What?

David   She has another man, Madeleine, my brother's wife... a lover... been going on for more than two years now...

Sarah   Who's the man? You?

David   When she meets her lover Johnny takes her in his car, drops her and then he buys a paper and sits in the car and reads the sports pages until she's finished. Or he drives back home and watches television or gets his fishing kit ready for the week-end or whatever and then drives back and picks her up. *Pause.* See what I mean?

Sarah   No.

Outside the compartment, in the corridor, the Guard, now quite clearly drunk, walks past, stops momentarily and tries to establish eye contact with Sarah.

Guard   I'll be back later, darling.

Sarah   All right.

The Guard continues to stagger along the corridor.

David   *slowly* Now, that says something about him. And about you. And me... What does it say though?

Sarah   David, I think you're drunk.

David   Darling... *Pause.* Darling... We shall never be apart again. You must never leave me. I can't ever get enough love, ever... Sarah, how are you doing? Incommunicado? *Pause.* Sarah, my love, are you deaf? *Pause.* You know, you never seem to hear what I say... The prompter who only hears the lines she chooses to hear. *Giggles.* Why don't you do something about your face? Get rid of those phoney tears. *Pause.* SARAH!

Sarah   Back and forth, all the time, arrogant one minute, 'Sarah, what's wrong?' the next. Over and over again... I get so tired of it... *Pause.* I'd like to tell you about something, about something that happened to me yesterday. A wonderful, wordless experience. But it was love.

David   The hiss of the guillotine, I can hear it. Shall I look up so I can watch the blade fall? Or bare my neck and bury my face so I can't see?

Sarah   I'd like to tell you about something. I'd like to tell you about something wonderful, something that happened to me yesterday. *Tells her story with the help of her body, bends her wrists, turning the insides of her palms downwards and baring her neck as before an execution.* It was on the underground, I was on the train going to the station... A couple of stops and a man got on. He sat down opposite me. Nice, but nothing special, not particularly good-looking, pretty ordinary in fact, and not all that young, about your age. A few minutes passed and then, suddenly, I felt his eyes on me, very, very gently, as if he was stroking me... When I looked up I looked straight into his eyes... And there was so much love there, so much longing... I felt like a little girl, very small, shy and self conscious... We just sat there, only the two of us... He didn't say a word and I didn't either and then I looked away... I knew that if he'd said 'Come, let's go' I would've got up and followed him... I know I would've... Three more stops and then he got up and walked out... That's all... But I don't think I'll ever forget it... I remember something you said once... the meaning of some words, you said, is that they can't be forgotten. That's their significance... I broke out of the walls of my loneliness, I soared high above, on the wings of love... *Pause.* But I know it's you I love. And when I saw you, running across the station towards me with that big plastic bag I felt so happy.

David   *very sad* Sarah, Sarah...

Sarah   *screams* I can't have anything, can I, you won't let me have anything! Not even one moment of closeness with a complete stranger! Not even three stops on the underground, ten minutes, at most, when for once I could feel I existed. You don't allow me to exist! *Now in tears.*

That's what you've done! I don't exist because you won't let me! Because there's only YOU! Me, I'm sick. Sick, sick, sick! I don't want to love you, please let me stop!

David But of course you're sick, Sarah, of course you are. I can hear it all the time, sometimes clearly, sometimes faintly but it's there, always there.

Sarah I'm not sick. I love you.

David See? See what I mean? *Smiles.*

Sarah belts him, as hard as she can and continues to hit him for some time. Long pause while she calms down. David goes 'ouch', 'ouch', 'ouch'.

Sarah There, serves you right too. *Pause.* I hope you'll die soon... I hope someone just walks in and kills you.

The Guard walks in, drunk, and without his uniform jacket.

David Hullo there mate, won't you sit down?

The Guard smirks.

David What d'you want?

The Guard sits down.

Guard I sit wherever I want. It's my train.

David Do by all means. Well, now that you're here, I s'pose it's just as well... that you're here.

Guard Joseph Tito not exist in Yugoslavia. Joseph Russian name. From Russian bible.

David Good. Very good.

Guard You not the first to get off train in the middle of the night. *Pause. To Sarah.* Feel like a glass of -

Sarah What?

Guard   Slivowic. A glass of Slivowic.

Sarah   I don't think so. *Looks quickly at David.* Yes, that would be nice.

Guard   Come on then. Can't stay here.

Sarah   Why? Why can't I?

Guard   I have transistor in my compartment.

David   Transistor?

Guard   Radio, little Christmas tree and old newspapers. You don't believe?

Sarah   Beg your pardon?

Guard   Bad radio. No dancing. No singing.

Sarah   I see. *Pause.* What does it do then?

Guard   Nothing. Just sit there. Silence. No words. Come and look!

Sarah   I'd love to... You won't leave me, will you?

Guard   *winks* Never.

David gets up, picks up his plastic bag, walks out into the corridor, opens the door and throws himself into the darkness outside. The train continues and rolls, slowly and desultorily into the grey, deserted station in Belgrade, surrounded by modern, recently built and functional looking housing estates. It is twenty minutes past seven in the morning. Sarah gets out, looking ravaged and exhausted, puts her luggage down, sits down on one of her suitcases and starts crying.

David comes walking along the railway track, his clothes torn and dirty, his face covered in scratches.

When Sarah sees him she gets up and starts running towards him. They embrace. She talks to him, gently and lovingly, but all that can be clearly heard is 'I'd love to, I'd love to... I'll never leave you again, never ever...'

He starts crying, and so does she, strong, powerful fits. A dark train rolls into the station, full of people, singing and laughing. It is bound for Rome.

155

Sarah *still crying and wiping away his tears* I'd much rather go to Rome... I hate Greece... Come on, come on... Hurry, hurry!...

Music, very loud : Come un cavallo pazzo, Viola Valentino, Paradiso, Prd 10304

...I'd love to, I'd love to... We'll never be apart again... I know exactly the sort of wedding dress I want...

Curtain down, then up again, swiftly.

He is happy, dances. She goes up to him and starts cutting him, his face and his body while he continues to dance.

The train stops.

Italian peasants on their way to Rome for the traditional Easter ceremonies, get on the train. Some carry lamb carcasses which they hang on the racks as if they were coats. One family open the door to Sarah and David's compartment and look in. David is lying on the floor, Sarah is on the seat. They shake their heads.

Curtain down swiftly.

Summer Nights

by

Agneta Pleijel

Translated by Mark James

Agneta Pleijel

Characters	Karna	the mother

Her daughters

	Gertrud	a teacher
	Magda	a musician, working for television
	Ulrika	an actress

	Frederick	a businessman, married to Gertrud
	Bror	a journalist, married to Magda
	Thomas	a writer, Ulrika's boyfriend
	Tanya	Gertrud and Frederick's daughter

The play is set in a summer house in the country, and in town. The time is the present.

PROLOGUE

Sound of waves. LIGHTS UP on Ulrika and Magda, sitting on the floor. Thomas stands behind them in the background. Calm. Sound of waves fades slowly.

Ulrika *quietly* Hello, I'm Ulrika. This is my sister. Well, one of them. Her name is Magdalena. That's Thomas behind me.

Thomas There are certain moments that will stay with you for the rest of your life. I'll never forget that picture of those two women sitting next to each other, and the sound of waves in the distance. For a brief moment time stopped.

Magda It sometimes happens that way. Suddenly things you thought were one big blur become crystal clear. And you just know the next step you take is going to change the rest of your life. And that was one of those moments. For them. And for me.

Ulrika So we'd better talk to each other again about what happened.

Thomas *turns around* Yes!

Magda takes out a cigarette and lights it.

Thomas *to Ulrika* It was last summer. You were spending the holidays with your family at their summer house. I came along, though we hadn't known each other that long, maybe a year or so. One day at the beginning of the holidays I was sitting at my desk writing. You came in. Maybe that's where we should start. You told me you wanted a baby. Yes, we should start there.

Ulrika now has her hands in front of her face. Thomas is silent. No-one speaks. Music, a gentle beat.

Magda *handing a cigarette to Ulrika* Ulli, I've got to go.

Ulrika takes it, slowly. Magda goes. Ulrika smokes the cigarette. Thomas moves towards her. She doesn't look at him, hesitates, then hands him the cigarette. He takes it. LIGHTS fade. Sound of waves again.

ACT ONE

In the country

Scene one

LIGHTS UP on a row of deckchairs. Bright sunshine. Gertrud, Bror, Frederick and Ulrika are all sunbathing, eyes closed. Karna is crocheting in her chair. Tanya is lying on a lilo, headphones on. Magda is standing to one side of them, with her violin, deeply engrossed in some sheets of music. Thomas is on a different part of the stage, at his typewriter.

Gertrud What a wonderful day. I can't believe it turned out to be so sunny.
Karna I'm sure it won't last.
Ulrika Oh Mum.
Karna That's what they said on the weather forecast.
Gertrud Incredible, isn't it? After all these years, here we are again, back in the summer house, all together.

Magda draws her bow tentatively across her violin.

Karna You're not going to start playing again, are you?

Magda picks up her stand and leaves. Karna watches, guiltily, as she disappears.

Bror *eyes still closed* What's for lunch, Freddie?
Frederick *half asleep* Mmm?
Tanya Dad, can you drive me down to the ferry? I'm going into town tonight.
Gertrud Ssshh. He's asleep. I'll drive you, if you really have to go.
Tanya *gets up and stretches* Great. *She leaves.*

They sunbathe in silence. After a while Ulrika gets up, puts on her beach robe and goes over to Thomas. LIGHTS DOWN on the others.

Scene two

Thomas is sitting at his typewriter. Ulrika enters.

Ulrika Am I interrupting?

Thomas *pleased to see her* No, of course not!

Ulrika *sits on his knee* What do you make of them, then?

Thomas Great....

Ulrika Silly question. *Looks at the typewriter.* What are you writing?

Thomas You really want to know?

Ulrika Of course.

Thomas Just then, I was trying to find the words for the way the light is filtering through the curtains.

Ulrika A poem?

Thomas A curtain shimmering in the summer wind. The light sparkling through for a split second....No, I'm just trying to get going.

He gets up and exercises his fingers.

Ulrika You know, I sometimes wonder....is it possible for two people to be in love, without really understanding each other?

Thomas Maybe you can only be in love when you don't really understand.

Ulrika Thomas, there's something I wanted to tell you.

Thomas Yes?

Ulrika Strange. My heart's beating faster, as if I'm frightened.

Thomas There's nothing to be frightened about. Just tell me....

Ulrika Thomas, more than anything else in the world, I want to have a baby.

Thomas *brief pause* Now?

Ulrika *smiling* Look, forget it. Let's talk about something else.

Thomas It's a bit sudden, isn't it?

Ulrika Really?

Thomas Does it have to be....I mean....it's just that....I really want to write this book, I've been trying to for so long.

Ulrika I know, I know. I want you to write it, too.

Thomas And....it's just that I can't bear the thought of having to change nappies again. Ulrika, I've been looking for someone like you for so long. *Brief pause.* We both a need a bit more time.

Ulrika I haven't got much time left.

Thomas Don't be silly.

Ulrika I'm not being silly. Soon I'll have no time left at all. I'm not twenty any more. It'll be too late soon.

Thomas That's rubbish.

Ulrika That's what you think.

Thomas Look, I've got two kids I hardly ever see. The divorce has come through, thank God. But I sometimes wonder if my own kids know who I am. What would I tell them? They'd think I'd swapped them for someone else.

Ulrika But you've done that already, haven't you?

Thomas Only her, not them.

Ulrika Look, just listen to me for a moment. Once I used to be worried sick about getting pregnant. *Brief pause.* I wanted so much out of life. I wanted to do something. I wanted to change the world. I went on demonstrations. I supported all sorts of causes. I had an abortion. I wanted to find out who I really was. I wanted to become a good actress. I had another abortion. I wanted to be free and strong and stand on my own two feet. But perhaps deep down I was scared. I got pregnant again. This time I wanted to have the baby. But I had a miscarriage. I was determined not to cry. I just carried on working. But you just can't keep hiding from life forever. Sooner or later you realize you have to face up to it. And all I want now is a child.

Thomas Ulrika, my dear Ulli, please. I'm not asking for much. Just a little more time.

Ulrika nods and goes. LIGHTS DOWN. LIGHTS UP on the others. Karna and Frederick are cooking. Sound of waves. Magda's violin starts up again.

Scene three

Karna on the beach. Sound of Magda's violin, gently, in the background.

Karna Last summer? What was it like? What happened? You really think I remember? I was in the way, as usual. Oh, I know they're all very nice to me, they really are. But I know I'm no use to anyone. I worried about Magda, I really did. She plays that violin so beautifully, but it always makes me so nervous. It's like when she was a child. I always thought then she only played when she was unhappy. Yes, I worried about Magda a lot. I knew she and Bror weren't getting on very well.

Sound of Magda's violin grows louder

Scene four

Frederick is cooking. Karna comes and sits next to him. Sound of Magda's violin. Stops abruptly.

Karna It's so beautiful.

Frederick Can you pass me that knife, please.

Karna *reaches for it* Bror's not back from town yet, and it's getting late!

Thomas *enters* Anything I can do?

Frederick You can lay the table in a minute.

Karna No, I'll do it.

Frederick You don't happen to be sitting on the oven-glove, do you?

Karna *looks, and finds it* Oh, so I am. Vanished, gone in a puff of smoke, as they say. That's certainly how it felt, too!

Thomas What ARE you talking about?

Karna The feelings, the pain!

Frederick Oh, I see.

Karna Do you know when I first came here? It was in the thirties. Seved, the girls' granddad, still had his workshop here, and Ester was alive. I remember her saying it was lovely to have me as a daughter-in-law. Dear Lord, what little time we're given just disappears, doesn't it. I'd just put up some new curtains in the kitchen when I found the letter in Gunnar's pocket....and then I knew what was going on. And the first thing she did - Louise, his new woman - was to take down my curtains and put up those over there. She wouldn't even let me come back to get my things. The girls didn't feel welcome any more, either. Her kids slept in their beds. So unfair. Twenty years of marriage and not once did he talk about all we'd built up together. *Ulrika comes in and puts her arms around Thomas.* In all these years, he hasn't even dared see me. But how can you split up with someone without sorting things out? You only become bitter, and with no-one to turn to you become so unbearable no-one wants anything to do with you. Yes, they had to put me away in the end. And when I was in hospital I don't really remember who was looking after the girls. But Gunnar didn't do a thing, of course.

Ulrika But Mum, I was the only one living at home. The others had already left.

Karna There, you see, I don't remember a thing.

Ulrika But it was twenty-five years ago, Mum.

Karna Well, they must have done something to me in hospital. Aren't you cold like that?

Ulrika A bit. It's getting chilly.

Karna You ought to put something on. How can you sort things out with someone who just disappears? I mean, you can't exactly put an advert in the paper, can you? 'Please come back and sort things out.' Not that I wanted him back. No, that's not it at all. It's just that we really should meet up again, just once, before we die. Just to look each other in the eye and say it wasn't all a big mistake. I mean, the girls grew up and did well, didn't they? You know what I'm getting at. Your life should mean something. You can't just look at the past as one big mistake, wipe it out and forget about it, you just can't!

Ulrika But when something's too painful to remember, isn't it better sometimes to forget?

Karna Forget, forget, forget! All everyone wants to do these days is forget. The past just doesn't mean anything any more. You just block it out. Please, don't ever bottle anything up - you'll only end up all bitter and resentful. Sort out your problems while you can, you two. And you, Frederick. Are you listening, Frederick?

Frederick Yes, yes, I'm listening. But where is everyone? The food's ready. Where have they all got to? Where's Gertrud?

Bror appears, in office clothes, looking tired.

Frederick Hi there, Bror! What's new in the big wide world?

Bror *throws the evening paper at Frederick* Trouble in the Royal Family, some new tax row, some new survey on our sexual habits. Nothing that would interest you. Come on, let's have a drink before dinner. *Leaves.*

Frederick Hey, don't be too long. Supper's ready. Got a cigarette, Ulli?

Karna I'll lay the table.

Karna goes off. Sound of Magda's violin in the distance.

Karna There she goes again.

Frederick Thanks. *Takes a cigarette.* What's up? You're looking a bit pale.

Ulrika I'm freezing.

Frederick *looks at the cigarette, then puts it in his pocket* Autumn's nearly here.

Ulrika Just my time of the month, I'm afraid.

Gertrud *enters, harassed, holding a carrier bag* Hello!

Frederick There you are. Where have you been?

Gertrud *tastes the food* You said we were out of beer and Magda had promised to drive in to town to buy some. But then off she went into the forest with her wretched fiddle again. So I had to go....it needs more salt. *Is about to put some in.*

Frederick *stops her* No don't!

Gertrud *passes him the cans of beer* Here. What IS the matter with her? Is she mad or drunk, or both? Either way, she doesn't seem to give a damn about anything.

Thomas That's a bit unfair isn't it?

Gertrud Is it? Well, I s'pose I wouldn't understand, would I? But that's the way it seems to me.

Ulrika Don't get so worked up. Thomas only meant you sounded a bit sharp.

Gertrud Sharp! She doesn't give a damn about her kids. Tanya has taken care of them all afternoon. I'm being sharp, am I, because I care about the kids? Well, I'm so sorry, I keep forgetting it isn't very fashionable these days to care about your kids. I'm sorry, but I do. That's just the way I am, I'm afraid.

Karna *comes back* Can someone please go and get her. Where's Bror?

Frederick Right, let's eat.

Ulrika 'Fashionable', what do you mean 'fashionable'?

Gertrud All I mean is, if you don't have any kids of your own, like you for instance, it's only normal to have other things on your mind.

Ulrika What exactly do you mean by 'other things'?

Gertrud But having four kids of my own and a load more at school, as I do, it's obviously much easier for me to see things the way kids do.

Sound of the violin stops.

Karna What are you talking about? You're not having an argument, are you?

Ulrika So what 'other things' do you think I've got on my mind, then?

Gertrud *shouts out angrily* Oh, how the hell should I know! Something intellectual or arty, I s'pose. I'm sure you have loads of extremely interesting opinions on life. I don't know, do I. All I know is you haven't got any kids, so you've got time for all that.

Ulrika Oh I see. It's because you've never had time for anything else that you're such a stupid cow, is it!

Ulrika leaves. Bror returns, whisky bottle in hand. Thomas tries to follow Ulrika, but Bror stops him, and hands him the whisky bottle.

Bror No, no. Come and have a drink.

Gertrud What on earth got into her?

Karna Bror, you must go and talk to Magda. All she does is hide herself away and play the violin.

Bror Well I can't hear her. Anyone for a whisky?

Tanya enters.

Tanya Dinner ready yet?

Gertrud Maybe I was being a little sharp. Was I, Frederick?

Frederick No, you're just tired and hungry. Let's eat. Bring your glasses with you. *Leaves.*

Karna Gertrud, someone has to go and get Magda.

Tanya I'm starving. Can we eat now? *Leaves.*

Karna Bror!

Bror Look, I do NOT want to go and get Magda. I want to eat, drink and be merry. Come on.

Bror takes the bottle from Thomas and leaves.

Karna But someone has to go and get her. She can't stay out there in the dark all on her own.

Thomas I'll go and get her. But I'd better fetch Ulrika first.

Karna pats him on the arm gratefully and leaves.

Gertrud *to Thomas* God, this place is a madhouse. Maybe I did sound a bit sharp, but I didn't mean to. Look, if I go and get Ulrika, you fetch Magda, alright?

Thomas and Gertrud go off in opposite directions.

Scene five

LIGHTS UP on Gertrud

Gertrud It was last summer. If we're going to talk about what happened, then I s'pose we'd better start there. What can I say? The place was a madhouse. I remember saying that all the time to Frederick, my husband. Didn't I, Frederick?

Frederick Yes.

Gertrud We were supposed to look after everything, you and me. The kids, Mum, the food, Magda. Whose bright idea was

169

it for us all to get together in the summer house in the first place?

Frederick Yours.

Gertrud Yes, yes, I know. But I really wanted us sisters to get together again like in the old days. Why didn't you tell me what a stupid idea it was, Frederick?

Frederick I did.

Gertrud bites her lip, nods. Frederick leaves.

Gertrud Anyway, last summer. There I was, on my way to say sorry to Ulrika, even though I hadn't said anything to be sorry about.

Gertrud leaves. LIGHTS UP on Thomas.

Scene six

On the beach. Magda, standing with her violin, looks out to sea, a bottle of wine in her hand. Thomas appears. It has now become dark.

Thomas *gently* Magda, Magdalena.

Magda What do you want? *Thomas doesn't answer.* I know you've come to tell me dinner is ready. *Thomas nods.* But I'm not hungry. So you might as well go. I know you're going to say....

Thomas ....that you can't stay out here in the dark, with your violin, all on your own....

Magda ....because Mum'll get worried and so'll Gertrud and Frederick, and we mustn't upset them, must we? Is Bror back yet?

Thomas Yes.

Magda What's he doing?

Thomas Your husband? He's drinking whisky.

Magda Look, why don't you go back to the house and tell Mum
I'm fine, but I'm not hungry, and all I'm doing is practising
on my violin, all right?

Thomas No.

Magda No?

Thomas No.

Magda Well, excuse me, but have you ever read the UN Human
Rights Charter?

Thomas *sits down* No.

Magda *tightens the screws on her violin, expertly* It states quite
clearly that every individual is born free, with the
inalienable right to a moment's peace and quiet, at least on
Thursday evening, out in the country. I'll be along later,
and I promise to be a good girl. But right at the moment I
just don't feel like facing Bror over dinner. So thanks for
being so sweet, but please go back. Right now I want to
be left alone.

Thomas Do you mind if I sit down here for a couple of minutes?

Magda Have you had an argument with Ulrika? .... Sorry, it's just
that I've had one with Bror. Well, argument is a bit of an
under-statement. I think we woke the whole house up.

Thomas Yes. You did.

Magda And what did you say when we met this morning?
'Morning Magda, sleep well?' *She walks a couple of steps.*
Everything's falling apart. We've come back to a house
that fell apart a long time ago. Mum fell apart, Dad fell
apart, and now it's my turn. I don't want the same to
happen to my kids, but how can I stop it?

Thomas But what makes you think your kids will fall apart?

Magda Bror and I are going to split up, and that'll hurt them badly.
But I really don't want to talk about that now.

Thomas I'll go now. But I'd really like to hear you play the violin.

Magda *changes her tone* I used to play quite well. I should've kept
it up. It's too late now. I wanted to get a proper job, so I
could support myself and be independent. And what am I
doing now? Churning out background music for television!

171

I've thrown away everything that ever meant anything to me. When I get home, I'm so tired, all I ever do is argue with Bror. What with the kids screaming, the television on full blast and never a moment's peace, who needs the violin?

Thomas And I wanted to write a book. But I got married instead. Two kids, a house, a mortgage, the lot. Then I met your sister, Ulrika - an actress, an artist. But what is art anyway? An illness that makes you cling to the truth, your own truth? The right to be seen for who you are? Is that why, suddenly, you know one day you just can't put it off any longer? But....

Magda But what?

Thomas Don't give up playing the violin, Magda, please don't give up.

Magda But what? What did you mean, when you said 'but....'?

Thomas You're so beautiful.

Magda Am I?

Thomas Yes.

They now stand close to each other. They kiss. Bror appears behind them. He watches. He sees Magda pulling away from Thomas.

Magda We should go now. Bror will be coming to get me.

Thomas He's drinking whisky.

Magda Then he'll definitely be here soon.

Thomas starts to pull her closer again.

Bror *whisky bottle in hand* He's here already. Look, please don't let me disturb you. Go on, kiss. I'll just stand here and watch.

Magda *brief pause* Please go Bror.

Bror *silkily* Well, Magda, my dear, you've changed your tune from this morning.

Magda You hurt me.

172

Bror And you rejected me.

Magda You want all of me, and that's more than I can give.

Bror So what've you got that's so special, then? So special, you've got to keep it all for yourself?

Magda You only want me so you can take me apart and see what's inside.

Bror Believe me, dear little Magda, I've been looking and looking for whatever it is that's supposed to be so special. If it's there, you're doing a bloody good job hiding it.

Magda So instead you get drunk and cheat on me.

Bror Oh, cheating is it, when you reject me?

Magda And what about you? You reject me, don't you, when you don't accept me for what I am.

Bror My dear Magdalena, who the hell do you think you are? Please tell me. I'm not good enough for you, is that it? After all, I'm just a burnt-out, middle-aged hack, working his arse off, right? And for what?

Magda Well, not for me, that's for sure. But what does it matter anyway? It's all over. *She runs off.*

Bror *calling after her* Over? It'll never be over, dear little Magdalena. You'll never face up to life, not on your own. And no-one else but me will ever put up with you!

Thomas and Bror alone. Bror swigs from the whisky bottle.

Thomas I kissed your wife.

Bror I noticed.

Thomas It was nice.

Bror I'm sure she'd agree.

LIGHTS DOWN on them. LIGHTS UP on Tanya.

173

Scene seven

Tanya is standing on stage, pumping up an air-bed.

Tanya Last summer? Nothing special about last summer. It was rather boring. I didn't have a job and I had a boyfriend, Samir. His father came from Tunisia. We broke up. That was July, or August. I liked Ulrika's new boyfriend. He was all right. There was something about him. He seemed to know what he wanted from life. I had a good mind to ask him what it was. I mean, it was pretty obvious the others had no idea what they wanted. You've only got one life, after all, but all they ever did was sit around on the beach, wittering on. I listened, but I can't say I learnt much from them. I seem to remember one afternoon, though. Thomas had swum right out to the red buoy at Lundkvist's jetty, and as he came up out of the water, Ulrika said, ' Well, hello there, my Ulysses.' So I had to go look it up in the library, because I didn't want to ask them who Ulysses was.

Scene eight

On the beach. Sunshine. Deckchairs and lilos. Thomas, in his swimming trunks, comes up out of the water. Tanya lifts her head up from her lilo, where she's lying, surrounded by magazines and with her headphones on.

Ulrika Well, hello there, my Ulysses.
Bror *lifts head up from towel* Ulysses?
Karna *looks up from her crocheting* Don't you know who Ulysses was?
Frederick He must do, he works for a tabloid. Famous Greek shipowner, married to an Italian opera singer.

Magda *joining in* That was Orestes, not Ulysses. I'm sure Bror
knows that.

Karna Orestes! Surely he wasn't called Orestes, was he Bror, the
one married to Maria Callas?

Bror No.

Karna Well what's he called then?

Bror What does it matter?

Karna But I'd like to know. Who was it Gertrud?

Gertrud Onassis, Mum.

Karna Onassis? But he was the one married to Jacqueline
Kennedy, wasn't he?

Tanya What ARE you all going on about?

Magda Do you know who Ulysses was, Tanya?

Tanya I'm reading.

Frederick Well, do you know who Onassis was?

Tanya I told you, I'm reading.

Karna *saddened* None of us knows anything.

Bror What the hell does it matter, anyway?

Gertrud *after a moment's silence* Isn't it wonderful the weather's
so nice today. I hate it when it rains, like last week. And
it's so nice we're all here together again. It does feel
strange, though, without the children.... now they're all
grown up.

Tanya But I'm here.

Gertrud Yes, but you're grown up too. More or less, anyway.
Don't you think it's strange, Frederick?

Frederick I think it's wonderful.

Gertrud Do you really?

Frederick *to Tanya* So who's this black chap you're seeing
tonight, then?

Tanya turns her back to him. Silence.

Gertrud This weather! Isn't it marvellous. Just think, it'll be winter
before long, so let's enjoy it!

Thomas It's difficult to think at all in this heat. Difficult to work, too.

Frederick It's great not to have to. I think my fish gratin must be almost ready.

Ulrika It's fascinating to listen to what people say when they really mean something completely different. Like when they say, 'Oh, isn't the weather nice' when they mean 'go to hell' or 'come and give me a hug'. That's what we call subtext in the theatre.

Frederick You actors have some pretty funny ideas about people.

Gertrud You certainly do. All I meant to say was the weather's wonderful.

Bror I won't have you say anything bad about actors, not in my company. After a hard day's work, going to the theatre's my favourite way of relaxing. I just sit there, and the actors come on stage and tell me all I need to know. How to live, how to love, how to vote. They're experts on all of these things. And if you don't watch out, they move in for the kill, jump up onto your lap to make sure you respond. They terrify me. What do they want from me? And what makes them think they know so much more about everything than I do?

Ulrika Oh come on, Bror!

Bror But you know so much more than I do, don't you?

Karna And you can't stand that, can you?

Magda He's just jealous.

Bror Too bloody right I am! No one's going to pay just to look at me, and I bare my soul and show my feelings all the time!

Frederick It might be worth paying you not to.

Magda *smiling* Definitely!

Karna Oh please don't start arguing again. We were having such a good time.

Bror Who's arguing? I'm just jealous. You too, eh Freddie?

Frederick *grins* Of course.

Ulrika Jealous of what?

Frederick In the theatre you show your feelings and everyone thinks it's all very interesting, and they all sit there, gawping at you. But I don't show mine, so I'm not the slightest bit interesting, am I? Ask anyone. I'm right, aren't I?

Bror Absolutely.

Frederick Put me on stage and the theatre would be empty in no time. That's how interesting I am.

Bror Too right.

Ulrika Wow! That'd be some audience reaction! What's your secret, Frederick?

Frederick *modestly* Oh it's nothing, really.

Thomas I'd like to know too.

Frederick Really?

Thomas How can you sit there boasting you're much more boring than anyone else? Is this some kind of competition?

Frederick *grins* I'm a decent, honest man. Is there anything more boring than that? I have the soul of a civil servant!

Thomas I didn't know they had souls.

Frederick Of a sort, yes.

Thomas And what sort is that?

Ulrika The sort that suddenly burst open....like Othello! And then....

Karna Othello? He was the one who was so jealous, wasn't he? And he was black, wasn't he?

Bror *growls* 'Black Man Murdered by Rifle-Wielding Civil Servant on Ostermalm.'

Karna But he was, wasn't he?

Ulrika Yes Mum. As black as the ace of spades.

Karna A Moor. The Moor's Last Sigh!

Frederick But I don't have a rifle.

Ulrika But jealousy, you know about that, don't you?

Frederick Not really. Sounds too much like hard work. I wonder how my gratin is getting along?

Ulrika 'Too much like hard work'! What's wrong with you? If your faithful, loving wife slept with someone else, what would you do then? With Bror, for example?

Frederick With Bror?

Karna What are you talking about, for goodness sake?

Bror Interesting thought, eh Gertrud?

Karna Now you stay out of this, Bror!

Bror That's exactly what Magda always says.

Karna And she's right.

Bror *flexes his muscles, poses* Go on, Ulrika.

Ulrika All I wanted to say was....no, forget it.

Thomas No, carry on. If Gertrud slept with Bror, Frederick....

Karna But you'd never do such a thing, would you Gertrud?

Frederick I'd be very, very surprised. But shooting him...?

Thomas If it was a question of your honour?

Frederick *laughs* My honour?

Thomas All right, so you don't have any. But tell us what you'd do, anyway. It'll help me with my book. What would Modern Man do in a situation like that? Come on Frederick!

Frederick What would I do? Well, I'd ask Gertrud what was going on. And what'd she say? What do people say in situations like that? Probably 'Look, really, it didn't mean anything. We had too much to drink and it just happened. I'm really sorry, Gertrud....'

Ulrika *listening attentively* You mean 'Frederick'.

Frederick Yes, yes, of course. 'Sorry Frederick,' she'd say. And I'd say, 'OK, Gertrud, let's not talk about it any more.' Something like that. I'm sorry, Thomas, but it's probably not exciting enough for your book, is it Gertrud?

Gertrud No, not really. Not very exciting at all.

Ulrika What do you mean, 'is it Gertrud?' How do you know what Gertrud would say?

Frederick Well, I suppose I don't.

Ulrika What if she said, ' We've been in love for years.' What would your reaction be then?

Frederick I'd be surprised, very surprised.

Ulrika Of course. You always are. But then what would you do?

Frederick What could I do? Nothing!

Ulrika You could cry, curse, fight for your love. You could shoot him....or her!

Frederick I'm afraid you're hoping for too much, Ulrika.

Ulrika But you love her, don't you? You've got to do something!

Karna What's all this? Bror, you mustn't be unfaithful to Magda, do you hear!

Bror What are you talking about, Karna?

Frederick You actors, you expect too much from us ordinary mortals. Why don't you stick to Shakespeare. There's enough people with interesting emotions there!

Karna Magda's unhappy, Bror, very unhappy.

Thomas No, you're wrong. If it was really like that, then people wouldn't be interested in their own lives any more, and that'd be awful. We're just like the characters Shakespeare wrote about. It's just that we don't realize it, because Shakespeare's not around to write about us. Someone should write something about you, Frederick. I'd really like to.

Frederick Thank you very much, Mr. Shakespeare. How do you do? Pleased to meet you.

Bror But why d'you want to write about Frederick? He's so boring. You'd be much better off writing about me instead, Tommy.

Frederick I'm worried about my fish gratin. I'm not too sure your wife's got the right touch with gratins. *Leaves.*

Bror Yes, why don't you write about me. I'm just like Macbeth, full of passions and imperfections. What do you reckon, Tommy? My dear little Gertrud. Pity, isn't it, that we've known each other for so long the magic's gone. Otherwise we could....you know....well, what do you think?

Karna *shudders* It's getting cold. *She leaves.*

Bror Look, Mum's gone now. Wouldn't it be exciting? What's wrong?

Gertrud *unhappy* What do you want me to say? I feel old all of a
sudden. And fat and ugly. Summer's almost gone, and we
all have to start waiting again. For what? All my life, it
feels like I've always been too late for everything.

Bror It's never too late, Gertrud, not for you and me!

Gertrud *very unhappy* Yes, precisely for you and me.

Bror Gertrud, my ever young, my beautiful, my curvaceous
Gertrud! *Strokes her cheek.* Let's go for it, even if it's just
to give Thomas a hand with his book.

Gertrud *bursts out angrily* It's almost autumn! And I'm not even a
good teacher any more. Why are you so horrible?!

She bursts out crying, gets up and runs off.

Ulrika *calls after her* Gertrud!

For a moment, everyone is quiet. Then Bror puts on his beach robe.

Tanya I don't understand. What are you doing?

Bror *his voice tired* My dear Tanya, what makes you think we
were doing anything?

*Bror leaves. Tanya looks at Thomas and Ulrika. She picks up her beach
robe and leaves.*

Scene nine

LIGHTS on Ulrika and Thomas. Thomas leaves.

Ulrika Well, the holidays came to an end. We all said our
goodbyes, and just me and Thomas were left in the
summer house. A cold wind was blowing in from the sea,
and the last sailing boats disappeared over the horizon.
The trees had all turned golden yellow, and in the forest

180

there was a strange echo. I'd asked Thomas a question at the beginning of the summer. He never answered me. I felt I couldn't live with his silence. So I left. Afterwards I kept thinking over and over again that it was wrong. But at the time I felt it was right.

Scene ten

LIGHTS UP on Thomas, sitting at his typewriter; on the table, a pair of binoculars and a wilted rose in a vase. He is wearing a big sweater. He is typing. Ulrika enters, and walks into Thomas' light. She is also dressed in autumn clothes.

Thomas So you're off? Where're you going?

Ulrika Arvidsjaur. We're shooting the outdoor scenes up there.

Thomas Arvidsjaur?

Ulrika Yes, the film's set in winter. The snow scenes are being shot in Arvidsjaur.

Thomas Not exactly next door, is it? This is all a bit sudden.

Ulrika You'll have all the time in the world for writing.

Thomas Ulrika, I don't need any more time. And I don't want you to leave.

Ulrika If you change your mind, let me know.

Thomas *bitter* That's the difference, isn't it? You want something from me. A child. And all I want is you. But I s'pose that's not enough.

Ulrika That's not true.

Thomas Isn't it?

Ulrika I'll tell you, if you'll listen. I'm the sort of woman men like to work with or make love to. I'm the sort of woman men like to discuss things with, be seen in restaurants with. But I'm not the sort of woman you stay and have children with....No, let me finish....I'm sorry, Thomas, but you're not the first man in my life. And with every single one of them there's always been something else. Wife, children, work, whatever, but never me.

Thomas You know, you're the best thing that's ever happened to me.

Ulrika I've wanted a child for many years, but you're the first person I felt I could say it to. It was like stepping out onto a swaying rope bridge, looking down into the abyss, thinking 'God, what if there's no one there on the other side to catch me if I fall?' And you weren't there waiting on the other side.

Thomas Ulrika!

Ulrika So I stumbled and fell and grasped for something to hold on to. That's why I have to work. That's why I'm leaving now.

Thomas But I am here. I was standing there on the other side. You just didn't see me.

Ulrika Summer's gone, and so's autumn, almost. I'm leaving.

Thomas But wait, we've got to talk about it.

Ulrika I don't want to hear any more. There's always something else. Something more important. Your children! Whatever! I just don't want to hear it all over again!

Thomas Ulrika, please don't go.

But she's already gone, leaving Thomas alone on stage.

Scene eleven

Thomas is seated at his desk. The binoculars and the wilted rose in the vase are still on the table.

Thomas And she just left. *Clearly upset.* Just like that, without even leaving a forwarding address. And then a postcard arrived, with some bloody Lapp on it - sorry, it was a perfectly ordinary Lapp - and the name and telephone number of some hotel in the middle of nowhere. But I didn't ring. I just sat here, looking out of the window at the lake outside the summer house. A thin layer of frost had started to form and suddenly everything became white, as though a deep slumber was falling over the whole countryside. *He picks up his binoculars and looks out.* I sent a postcard. I only wrote two words: 'Come back.' She didn't. So I carried on writing. Weeks went by, but nothing happened. I carried on writing. But no-one phoned, no-one came by.

Bror enters, dressed in winter clothes.

Bror Except me. You forget, I came to give you a hand beaching the boat. And I did a couple of weeks worth of washing up, though I doubt you even noticed my efforts. *Throws his gloves on the table.* I was even going to give that dead rose of yours some fresh water. But you wouldn't let me. *He goes to take the rose from the vase.*

Thomas No, leave it. *Stops him.*

Bror It's seen its best days, I'd have thought. All right, all right. I'm off then. What's that you're writing? *He takes a piece of paper from the desk.*

Thomas *trying to get it back* No, give it back.

Bror *holds on to it, fending him off* It's a poem.

Thomas Give it back.

Bror *reading* 'In front of me, a rose in a vase.'

Thomas Look, I said give it back.

Bror Shut up. 'In front of me, a rose in a vase. For three weeks I've watched it slowly die. A sad, tragic and frighteningly human death.' *Pauses, then continues.* 'But I still don't know the exact moment it happened.'

Thomas I don't like other people reading my work.

Bror You pompous prat.

Thomas It's private.

Bror Private, eh? Don't talk to me about writing. I write too, you
know. Yes, for 500,000 readers. And what do I write?
Crap, utter crap.

Thomas But that's your job. You're good at it.

Bror But has it ever occurred to you that I might've wanted to
write something else. I did you know.

Thomas What did you want to write, then?

Bror Anything. As long as it was true.

He gives the poem back to Thomas.

Bror We can't go on living like this. Anyone with eyes that see and
a heart that feels knows it. We're the living dead. We died
in mid-life, without even noticing it. *He starts to leave,
then turns round and smiles.* That rose, Tommy, that's me.
You're writing about me. Take it easy. *He leaves.*

Thomas And I stayed there in the summer house, alone. It was
late autumn.

Thomas starts writing. Music.

Scene twelve

*Music stops. Tanya is standing behind Thomas, suitcase in her hand,
smiling broadly.*

Tanya Hi!

Thomas Tanya? Where did you come from?

Tanya From town, of course, where d'you think? Is it okay if I
stay a few days?

Thomas What, here?

Tanya *smiles* Yes, here. Listen, I'm going to take a sauna. *She
leaves.*

Thomas *calling after her* Do Gertrud and Frederick know you're
here?

Tanya *off-stage* Don't talk to me about them. All Frederick ever
does is nag me about getting a proper education. I mean,
I've stayed until I was sixteen and I've taken God knows
how many courses. How many more do they expect me to
take? Why should I study anyway? It's not for me. I'm just
not cut out for it. And they know it, too. They're just
pretending. Plans for the future, that's all they ever talk
about.

Thomas What are your plans then?

Tanya Plans? *Re-enters.* Why d'you always have to plan? It's not
healthy, you know.

Thomas But Gertrud and Frederick are only thinking of you getting
a good job, and....

Tanya Give it a rest, please! That's exactly what's so unhealthy.
I just want to live! There's enough money in this country
to go round, right? Everyone can get what they need, if
they really want to, can't they?

Thomas I s'pose so.

Tanya It's just seems so stupid, killing yourself, doing something
you really don't want to do, when there are people around
without jobs, who'd love to do it instead! I'm fed up with
it all, and I'm fed up with living at home. But Frederick
won't help me get a flat, 'though I know he could if he
wanted to.

Thomas But that means paying rent, and....

Tanya I know, I know! *Smiles.* I know I'm going on and on about
it! Throw me out, if you want, along with everything else
you don't need!

Thomas *laughs, touches her* Tanya!

Tanya *looks at him* You're not like all the others. That's why I
came.

LIGHTS change. Thomas and Tanya are now sitting on the sofa.

Tanya It's so quiet here.

Thomas I'm trying to write about this house.

Tanya You write about houses?

Thomas Not just about this one. About old houses, about the old days. The way people used to live. The tools they had. The whole history of the place. There's not enough history in our lives any more. *He shows her Seved's plane.* Look at this old plane I found in the shed. It must've belonged to your great grandfather.

Tanya Seved.

Thomas Yes, Seved. It's part of our history, too. They must have worked hard, far too hard. But they knew they were doing something useful. They knew there were boundaries to their lives, to what they could and couldn't do. Where are ours? They still exist, of course, but they're just not clear any more, are they?

Tanya So you're writing a book about old tools, then?

Thomas *gives a little laugh* No, about us.

Tanya About us?

Thomas Yes, in a way.

Tanya About me, as well?

Thomas In a way, yes.

Tanya Where's Ulrika?

Thomas Ulrika. She's not here. She's left.

Tanya When's she coming back?

Thomas I don't know. She had to go away.

Tanya Are you upset?

Thomas shrugs his shoulders. Tanya puts her arms around him. They caress, then kiss, and end up making love. When the LIGHTS go UP again, they are lying next to each other. Tanya is asleep. Thomas wakes up. He looks at her and tries to free his arm. She wakes up. They look at each other.

Tanya *gently* I do believe in love.

Thomas What do you mean?

Tanya You asked me about my plans, what I wanted. I said I didn't want anything, really. But I do believe in love. If I said that at home, they'd just laugh. But I know I can say that to you.

Thomas *gently* What do you think love's about, then?

Tanya It doesn't have to be about anything, does it? It just happens, doesn't it? Does that sound terribly naive?

Thomas No.

Tanya It's being close to someone. That's what I want. I want to be close to someone I like very, very much, every day and every night. I know work's important, and all that, but I don't think about it much. It'll all sort itself out in the end. No, I want it to be like we're sharing the same skin. That's how close I'd like to be. That's what love's about and that's what I want. Do you think it could be like that?

Thomas Yes, for you, maybe. But not for everyone.

Tanya But that's what I want.

Tanya snuggles up to Thomas. His eyes are open. LIGHTS fade.

Scene thirteen

LIGHTS UP on Thomas's desk. He paces up and down, looks at the paper in his typewriter, tears it out and throws it away. He is restless. It is close to midnight and his writing lamp is on. He dials a number. LIGHTS on Ulrika. She is in a hotel room and is woken up by the phone ringing. She fumbles for the phone, which is underneath a ski-ing poster.

Ulrika *very drowsy* Yes?

Thomas Come back! I miss you so much! Hello? Are you there?

Ulrika Thomas!

Thomas I've been a fool. Can you hear me?

Ulrika *she starts to smile* Yes!

Thomas *as loud as he can* I want to be with you all the time! Can you hear me?

Ulrika Yes, yes, but not when you're shouting!

Thomas Well, listen then. I want to have children with you, Ulrika, loads of them. I want to work with you, make love to you, live with you, tell you off when you're being silly, comfort you when you're unhappy and bring you breakfast in bed! Please, Ulrika, come back! Are you still there?

Ulrika Yes!

Thomas Say something then!

Ulrika I can't. I'm crying.

Thomas Don't cry, life's too short. Just tell me, yes or no.

Ulrika *as loud as she can* YES!

Thomas That's settled then! Are you coming home now? Right away?

Ulrika Yes, yes, I'm coming.

Ulrika hangs up the receiver, fetches her boots from underneath the bed, puts on her big fur cap and knitted gloves, while she continues to talk to the audience....

Ulrika Well, I didn't exactly go right away, it wasn't as easy as that. It took quite a while to sort everything out, and during the last few days of shooting it felt as if I was in a trance. I must have looked a complete idiot. We even had to do some stupid re-shoots just because of me. But then, at long last, I was on my way....

Ulrika disappears, then re-appears in a night-shirt, fur-cap and knitted gloves, torch in her hand, at the summer house....

Ulrika ....and at long last, I was back with Thomas in the summer house.

They embrace. He helps her off with everything except the night shirt, and then they are back together on the sofa.

Ulrika That night when you rang ... why that night?

Thomas I don't know. But it had to happen sometime.

Ulrika Yes, but if you hadn't rung that night....

Thomas But I did. It was just a matter of time.

Ulrika ....then we might've lost each other forever.

Thomas Never. That would never have happened, and you know it.

Ulrika It might have. Weeks went by and it was beginning to feel like you were on another planet. That's how far away you felt.

Thomas Let's not talk about it any more.

Ulrika So far away, that once I was unfaithful to you.

Thomas *brief pause, then smiles* No you weren't, not really. But tell me about it in the morning and then I might believe you and give you what for. But right now, Ulrika, we simply don't have time to waste.

Ulrika *smiles as well* You're right, you're so right, my darling. We simply can't waste any more time.

They begin to make love. And then the telephone rings.

Thomas Let it ring.

Ulrika No, it's probably Mum, wanting to know where we're going to spend Christmas. Tell her I'll ring her back.

Thomas *answers phone* Yes?

Tanya appears, wearing her overcoat, telephone receiver in hand.

Tanya Thomas! You'll never guess what! We're going to have a baby! You know, I could hardly believe it when the doctor told me the tests were positive, but it's true! And I know what I'm going to call him already. Are you there, Thomas?

Thomas Yes, I'm here.

Tanya I've never been so happy in all my life, Thomas! Come over, you must. You've got to be here when I tell Mum and Dad. Are you coming? Can you come straight away?
Thomas I can't.
Tanya So when are you coming?
Thomas I'll come as soon as I can.
Tanya You promise?

LIGHTS off Tanya. Thomas goes back to Ulrika

Ulrika What was all that about?
Thomas Oh, nothing important.
Ulrika *looking at him* Last night, what I said, did I upset you?
Thomas *shakes his head* Look, Ulrika, there's one thing I'd like you to know. I've always loved you, from the very first moment I saw you. It just took a while before I realized quite how much.

Thomas kneels down, buries his head in her lap. Ulrika smiles. She is happy. LIGHTS DOWN.

Interval

ACT TWO

In town

Scene fourteen

In the editorial office. The night-shift. Moonlight. Gentle throb of printing press. Bror at his desk. Thomas in his overcoat, typewriter at his feet.

Thomas That's how it is.

Bror *after a brief pause* Well, what do you expect me to do about it?

Intercom Bror, we're putting the front page to bed. Will you be long?

Bror *pushes the intercom button* I said I was busy, didn't I? Do what the hell you like. Just as long as the paper comes out and you don't bring down the government! *Pushes the button again.* On second thoughts, why not! *Aside.* 'Bout time they learnt no-one's indispensable. *He pulls out a whisky bottle and a plastic cup.* Little bribe from one of the unions! Go on, have a drink.

Thomas But how the hell could it have turned out like this? Tell me how?

Bror You know what really puzzles me about the way people think, nowadays? It's not that people are screwing around - they've always done that. No, it's that they're so bloody surprised that this might result in the birth of a baby. I mean, in the old days people were under no illusions that one thing might lead to another!

Thomas But why her!

Bror *aggressively* Let me try and guess. That special way she crossed her arms, maybe? Those curves beneath her bikini, as she lay on the beach last summer? A glimpse of a nipple as we got out of the sauna? That pert behind or maybe it was those firm thighs?

Thomas That's enough!

Bror Well, you asked me. How do I know? Maybe the shadow of her smile?

Thomas It can't be as simple as that.

Bror Not as romantic, no. But simple all right.

Thomas is silent.

Bror Frankly, I'm far more interested to know why Tanya went to bed with you.

Thomas *bursts out* I don't want her to have it!

Bror You know, the most remarkable things happen all the time and no- one's the slightest bit surprised. If you press a button, there's light, just like that! And if you turn on a tap, water comes out right through the wall! People go to America, or even to the moon - through the air! You can find out the most intimate things about your neighbour simply by logging in to a computer. No-one's surprised by all that. But if someone you're having lunch with goes off and dies, or some woman gets herself pregnant, then it comes as a hell of a surprise. You know what I think? I think because it's within our power whether this planet survives or not, we believe we've got control over life and death too. But we haven't you know. Nature's still ahead. Maybe one day it'll happen. 'O fons Bandusiae, splendidor vitro' Horace - maybe one day we'll conquer nature, but right now she's just that little bit ahead. And if you ask me it's a bloody good thing too, cos I don't trust us. I don't like the sort of things we get up to. You might not agree with me right now, but think about it - certain things should be left exactly as they are, Tommy.

Thomas *after a brief pause* Thanks for those kind words, Bror, especially the bit from Horace.

Bror Don't mention it.

Intercom Just wanted to let you know Bror, the Russians are coming. It's World War Three Sandgren says.

Bror *pushes the intercom button* Tell Sandgren we surrender.

Intercom He says you'll be shot for deserting.

Bror *about to answer, but changes his mind* But she wants the child, doesn't she?

Thomas That's what she says.

Bror How the hell can you tell her to get rid of it, then? *Shakes his head, changes his tone.* Why don't you want a kid, anyway. They're great. I love them.

Thomas But what about Ulrika? And me?

Bror looks up at Thomas, without answering.

Thomas *gets up* I'd better get going.

Bror Yes, if there's another World War on, they might need me in the main office.

Thomas I'm sure they will. Well, thanks for all your sympathy and advice.

Bror Oh, go to hell!

Thomas I will. That's exactly where I'm heading.

Bror Give my love to Ulrika.

Thomas She doesn't know about any of this.

Bror What! Were you planning to tell her, or are you waiting till she hears about it from Frederick? Or doesn't it matter? It's all in the family, after all.

Thomas Don't worry, I love Ulrika. But I guess you wouldn't understand that, would you.

Bror Someone ought to clock you one, you know.

Thomas Thanks a lot.

Bror Tommy, you don't know how cut-up I am about you and Ulrika. I could cry my eyes out.

Thomas nods, then leaves.

Scene fifteen

LIGHTS UP on Bror and briefly on Thomas. LIGHTS UP on Magda.

Bror When I got back that night, Magda was still awake. She looked up and saw something in my face, something she recognized.

Magda Pain.

Bror So she asked me what was up, and I told her.

Magda Ulrika and Thomas! I've got to go over there!

Bror No, Magda, there's nothing we can do.

Magda And I sat there in bed for a long time, waiting for daybreak. But it didn't come. The wet snow hit the window and a ray of light flickered in the December darkness. But that was all. Then morning came. And then evening.

Scene sixteen

Candlelight. When stage LIGHTS go UP Tanya is sitting on the floor, her nose a bit red. She is trying, somewhat clumsily, to wrap Christmas presents. Thomas is standing next to her in his overcoat.

Thomas *looking around* Great flat.

Tanya *snuffling* Dad found it.

Thomas Oh, right.

Tanya Why didn't you call?

Thomas I'm sorry.

Tanya I knew you'd come, though. Mum and Dad are really upset. But I'm on your side. They've got to realize I'm an adult now. When I get some furniture in here, it'll look much better. I'll decorate it and make it really nice. I know the sort of furniture that'll look just right, and I've already seen the cot I want.

Thomas Tanya, you and I have really got to talk.

Tanya Gertrud and Frederick are coming over soon. They want to talk to you.

Thomas Tanya, this is all a bit silly, isn't it?

Tanya What do you mean?

Thomas Aren't you at all interested in what I think about this?

Tanya Of course I am.

Thomas Or what Ulrika thinks.

Tanya *looks away* That's got nothing to do with me.

Thomas Hasn't it? And how'd you feel if I said the baby had nothing to do with me?

Tanya What do you mean?

Thomas You heard....I'm sorry, I'm sorry!

Tanya You're trying to get out of it, aren't you!

Thomas No, of course I'm not.

Tanya But you can't, you just can't, you know.

Thomas Tanya, my dear little Tanya, please listen. This can't be the way you wanted things to turn out. You wanted to love someone, and be so close it'd be like sharing the same skin. That's what you told me. You didn't want this.

Tanya Well I'll just have to accept it like it is, won't I?

Thomas Look, one day you'll meet someone you love, and you'll marry and have kids and everything will be just the way you really want it.

Tanya You want me to get rid of it, don't you! You want to turn me into a murderer! Never! Do you understand? Never! I want my child to have a father, and I want that father to be you, because it IS you!

Thomas But what if I don't want to be that father, Tanya?

Tanya One day you'll be as happy about our child as I am, I know it.

Thomas And what about Ulrika?

Tanya There's always the summer house. We can meet up with the rest of the family in the summer house, can't we? You, me, the baby, and all the others.

Thomas, dumbfounded, is unable to speak.

> **Tanya** *cajoling him* You just need a little time to get used to it.
> That's what Dad always says. Give it a bit of time and
> you'll get used to everything.
> **Thomas** 'Get used to it'! If that's what your Dad thinks life's all
> about, I don't think he's got it quite right, somehow.
> **Tanya** *brief pause, then cheerily* Don't you want to know what I
> think we should call him?

*Before Thomas has time to answer, Gertrud and Frederick are standing
there. Gertrud has a carrier bag, Frederick a Christmas tree.
Embarrassed silence.*

> **Thomas** *in an attempt to break the silence* Hello there, sorry about
> all this, eh....*laughs uncomfortably* ....but there's no need
> to look like that. I mean, you have to look at the funny side
> of it....But....I'm sorry....
> **Gertrud** So what are you going to do about it?
> **Thomas** What do you mean?
> **Gertrud** Exactly what I said. What are you going to do about it?
> *Sarcastically, when Thomas doesn't answer.* I mean, are
> you planning to move in together?
> **Thomas** But Gertrud....!
> **Gertrud** Well how should I know? I don't know anything, do I. I
> know you couldn't be bothered to call Tanya for weeks.
> But that's all. I knew nothing about you two. I was under
> the mistaken impression that you and Ulrika were a
> couple.
> **Thomas** We are.
> **Frederick** So what does she have to say about all this, then? Does
> she think it's all a joke, as well?
> **Thomas** I don't know what Ulrika thinks.
> **Gertrud** You mean she doesn't know?
> **Thomas** Not yet.

Gertrud Well, now you can forget about Ulrika. I know her. She's too proud. But I want to know what you plan to do about all this. Tanya is our daughter, you know. Why did you do it? What did you have in mind?

Thomas 'Have in mind'?

Gertrud Yes.

Thomas Nothing.

Gertrud So why did you do it then?

Thomas Why? Because there was a lot of affection there, between us. I was fond of her. And then it just happened. Is that really so strange?

Gertrud And you never thought about the consequences?

Thomas No I didn't. I honestly didn't.

Frederick That's enough Gertrud. Screaming and shouting won't get us anywhere.

Gertrud But he fooled her into thinking he cared!

Frederick Gertrud!

Thomas Of course I care about her, Gertrud! But why don't you ask Tanya what she 'had in mind'? This isn't the Middle Ages, you know!

Gertrud Tanya's just a child! But you didn't care enough to let that bother you, did you.

Thomas You're wrong Gertrud. Tanya's no child.

Frederick You bastard! It's all good material for your book, isn't it? You don't care about us at all. All you care about is whether we've got any 'interesting' feelings. Do you think I don't remember! What would happen if Gertrud went to bed with Bror! What would I do about it! Nice little party games on the beach, eh? Well tell me, what would happen if Thomas went to bed with Tanya? Just another party game? You're a fine one to talk about feelings! You've haven't got any, have you? All you do is write about life, the rest of us poor sods have to live it! And it's no bloody party game for us any more. Tanya's our daughter. And I want to know what you plan to do about all this!

Thomas What do you think I should do....?

Frederick You might think I'm living in the Middle Ages, but I think you should take responsibility for what you've done.

Thomas How? You mean marry Tanya, and....

Frederick Yes, why not? Hasn't the thought ever crossed your mind?

Thomas No.

Tanya Mum, Dad, please. Can't you go now?

Frederick *takes no notice* No. Exactly. And I suppose you deny it was you who led her on?

Thomas 'Led her on'? Tanya, you don't think I led you on, do you?

Tanya Please, can't you all leave. Please.

Frederick You bastard!

Thomas For God's sake, Frederick, we hardly know each other. We've absolutely nothing to base a marriage on.

Frederick Nothing to base a marriage on! Yes you have, you've got a child! *Throws the Christmas tree at Thomas.* It's so bloody simple, but everyone seems to have forgotten that! Do you think it's always been easy for me and Gertrud? Of course not. It's been difficult, and there were lots of things we had to give up. But we did it. We stuck together, because we had children together. Isn't that right, Gertrud?

Gertrud Yes, Frederick, we stuck together. Now please stop.

Frederick *to Thomas* And I'm proud of that. Everyone else has split up, for one reason or another, but not me and Gertrud. No, not us.

Silence.

Thomas *sad and tired* What can I say? What do you want me to say?

Frederick *sad and tired* There, Tanya, you see. That's exactly what we told you last night, isn't it? Just like we said.

Tanya I don't care what you said last night.

Gertrud Tanya, dear, Dad and I, we'll do everything we can to help you.

Tanya Stop it! I don't want to hear any more! It's like I wasn't
even here. No-one bothers to ask me what I want, not
even him. And I don't want him. But I want him to pay.
Gertrud Tanya, I ....
Tanya Look, both of you, just leave now, please.
Gertrud Come on Frederick.

They leave.

Tanya You're going to pay, you know.
Thomas How much?
Tanya A lot.
Thomas *tired* All right, Tanya, all right.

Thomas gets up to leave.

Tanya Thomas, I liked you, that's why it happened. I thought you
liked me too.
Thomas I did, Tanya. And I still do.

Thomas leaves.

Scene seventeen

*LIGHTS on Ulrika, lying on the sofa in her flat, reading a script. Thomas
enters, in his overcoat.*

Ulrika Something wrong? You know this is a great play.
Thomas I've got something to tell you. What are you reading?
Ulrika A play. Why are you looking at me like that?
Thomas Because I'm thinking. Or at least I think I am.
Ulrika Thinking about what, darling?
Thomas Well, I was wondering what we might be doing, you and
I, on New Year's Eve, the year Two Thousand.

Ulrika Twenty Hundred, you mean.

Thomas What?

Ulrika Isn't it supposed to be Twenty Hundred, not Two Thousand?

Thomas Whatever, we've got to decide whether we're going off to the Bahamas, or staying at home. There's bound to be some good films on the telly that evening.

Ulrika Are we going to be together then, you think, in the year Two Thousand?

Thomas Of course we are. Don't you think so?

Ulrika *laughs* That's sweet of you, making plans for New Year's Eve in the year Two Thousand.

Thomas Twenty Hundred.

Ulrika What was it you were going to tell me?

Thomas I love you and I just can't imagine life without you.

Ulrika Now you're making me nervous.

Thomas You know that's true, don't you?

Ulrika Yes, yes of course. But what are you really trying to tell me? There's been somebody else, hasn't there?

Thomas Yes.

Ulrika When?

Thomas A long time ago.

Ulrika I knew it! That night, when I told you what happened when I was away filming, there was something in your eyes. I'm right aren't I? It happened when I was away, didn't it?

Thomas Yes.

Ulrika So why didn't you tell me then? ....Well, maybe you were right not to. It was all in the past, before we really knew what we were doing.

Thomas Yes.

Ulrika So why are you telling me now?

Deadly silence.

Ulrika It's still going on, is that it?

Thomas No, it's over. Definitely.

Ulrika Are you sure?

Thomas Yes.

Ulrika So why ARE you telling me now, then?

Thomas When you were away, last autumn, Tanya suddenly appeared at the summer house.

Ulrika *incredulously* Tanya!? What! You jumped into bed with Tanya?

Thomas Yes, I'm afraid that's exactly what happened.

Ulrika *with mounting anxiety* I see, and now she's fallen in love with you, poor girl. Is that it? And you don't know what to do about it. Is that it?

Thomas Not exactly.

Ulrika Well what is it then?

Thomas Then she phoned one day. She's pregnant.

Ulrika WHAT? What are you saying? You mean you and Tanya are going to have a child?

Thomas Yes.

Ulrika gets up. Thomas tries to put his arms around her, but she pushes him away, maybe even hits him. He tries again, but she grabs her coat, trying to run out. He finally gets hold of her.

Thomas Where are you going?

Magda *off stage* Hello, it's me.

She enters.

Magda Where are you going?

Ulrika Out.

Magda Please Ulli, stay. I know. That's why I'm here.

Ulrika Oh, I see. You know, do you. Am I the only one who doesn't know? What is this, some sort of family gathering? Is Mother about to arrive? Shall I set the table and put the coffee on? *To Thomas.* Have you told everyone?

Thomas I only told Bror.

Magda And he told me. But no-one else knows. Well, apart from Gertrud and Frederick, of course. But Mum doesn't know, I'm sure she doesn't.

Ulrika Who can be sure of anything any more, Magda?

LIGHTS DOWN

Scene eighteen

LIGHTS on Ulrika and Magda. Thomas in the background.

Ulrika The pain. It comes from deep down inside me. Deep, deep down. And I know it'll get even worse, like a vein's been cut. My heart's pumping and pumping and every heartbeat sends floods of blood into my body. It's like I'm drowning inside!

Magda Ulli. Dear, dear Ulli.

Ulrika It just can't be true. But it IS. A child, HIS child. And as long as I'm alive, it'll be alive too. It'll have a name, and it'll see and hear. The pain. I just can't stand it!

Magda Let it hurt, Ulli!

Ulrika But how can you say that? It's so bad, and it's getting worse. I'm scared. I don't know what to do. I want to escape, but I can't.

Magda Pain is cruel, but you have to accept it. Pain is like a knife. When it cuts, it hurts. But it only hurts because you're alive. That's why you've got to welcome it.

Ulrika Welcome it?! You must be crazy. It's brutal. It's barbaric. It's sickening. A child! You don't know how much I'd give for a child. But I know I'll never have one. Instead, this child will live. I don't want this child to be born. I want it to die!

Magda Ulli!

Ulrika God, why do we do it? Why do we spend all our lives on our knees, crawling through the mud?

Magda Yes, blind to everything around us, until one day something happens. And up there, there's no help. Nothing but polluted air, television aerials, and our own anxiety. Then, suddenly something hits us right between the eyes, and it hurts. And for a brief dazzling moment the sky opens up, and everything's clear. Like now, Ulli. Suddenly it all makes sense, precisely because it's so painful.

Ulrika But I'm falling, can't you see I'm falling. Everything's breaking up inside me. Shards of glass everywhere, cutting into me. Please help me, somebody please help me!

Thomas gets up, moves closer.

Thomas Ulli, Ulli!

Ulrika Don't you dare touch me!

He leaves.

Ulrika All the time, there's a child growing inside her. It should've been mine, Magda!

Magda I know. But it isn't. It's someone else's child. Of course it hurts. The problem is that we don't know pain any more, just like we don't know life any more. We're living dead. We don't live. We don't feel any more. Remember, Ulli?
  'Can you feel the pain, She's strong and powerful. With her fists secretly clenched, She gives us all we crave, Our joyous souls, Our mysterious desires.'

Ulrika What's that? Who said that?

Magda Remember? You weren't very old at the time. Dad had left us, and Mum was crying, and then she got ill. I had to come home and look after you. I read to you from Edith Södergran's poems, to make you feel better. To make myself feel better too, probably. I kept reading them to you, over and over again.

'Can you feel the pain, She gives us life,
Love, solitude, and the face of death.'

You probably didn't understand much at the time. You were just a child. But the sound of the words was comforting for you. Remember?

Ulrika All I remember is wanting love and affection, not solitude and the face of death!

Magda No one would want that.

Ulrika Magda, it's like I'm really seeing you for the first time. Where have you been?

Magda And you, where have YOU been all this time?

Ulrika But if I don't run away, if I accept the pain, if I stay with him, even though it hurts so much....no....I can't do it.

Magda But he's hurt too.

Ulrika I hope so. God how I hope so.

Magda He didn't want it to happen.

Ulrika But he did it!

Magda He didn't think.

Ulrika *sarcastically* He didn't think.

Magda Some people think too much.

Ulrika What do you mean?

Magda Love's not within everyone's reach.

Ulrika No, Magda, just think about it. What about Tanya? And what about Gertrud and Frederick. No, it's impossible.

Magda What about Tanya? She'll survive, she's young and strong. She'll get over it. As for Gertrud and Frederick, well you don't need to worry about them. They'll be grandparents. They'll love that, now that their own kids have left home.

Ulrika You're crazy.

Magda Maybe, or maybe I'm not.

Ulrika Completely out of your mind.

Magda Yes, that's what Bror always says.

Ulrika You should've left him a long time ago, you know.

Magda Should I? *Lights a cigarette.* It's taken me years to make him understand that he'll never understand me. That may not be all that far from love.

Ulrika *after a brief pause* We'd better tell each other everything, all over again.

Thomas *turning* Yes!

Magda *looks at them, gives Ulrika her cigarette* Ulli, I must go.

Ulrika *takes the cigarette* Bye.

Magda leaves, Ulrika smokes. Thomas moves closer to her. Without looking at him, she hands him the cigarette. He takes it. Sound of waves. Roar of sea. LIGHTS fade, slowly.

Scene nineteen

Sound of water and waves, like the opening scene. LIGHTS UP on Gertrud.

Gertrud Winter came and went. I lay beside Frederick in bed, but I couldn't sleep. I told him I wished I was a child again, back in the summer house before Dad left. I wanted to be walking barefoot on the beach in a cotton dress, my hair in a clip, looking for nice round pebbles. Soon summer was with us again. When it was time to go on holiday, we all said to Mum that of course she had to come with us this summer, too. And so we drove out to the summer house.

Sound of waves returns. Gertrud and Frederick disappear.

Scene twenty

In the country

LIGHTS UP on the beach, as in Scene 1. Deckchairs and lilos, as before. Sound of waves grows faint. Karna is sitting on a chair, crocheting. Bror is reading a paper, Magda a sheet of music. Suddenly Karna sees the swans.

Karna Look, the swans. Look, Magda, they've got five little ones this year. How did they manage that?

Magda *absent-mindedly* Yes, Mum....

Karna What did you say?

Bror Magda says they must've been at it, those long winter nights.

Magda *affectionately* Oh stop it.

Bror *turning the page of his paper* Nature can be both gentle and generous. Nature has smiled on those swans, Karna.

Karna *returns to her chair* Yes, but whatever Nature gives, it takes back. When I looked in the mirror this morning, I was horrified. Why can't we get pretty new leaves every year, like the trees? I'd be a lime tree, if I could choose. They're my favourite. *Glares at the pine trees.* I hate pine trees. *Sighs.* Oh well, it doesn't really matter, does it? The times we live in, a bomb could drop on us any minute, couldn't it?

Magda *miles away* Mmmmm....

Karna That's what we've got to remember when we need cheering up.

Bror Yes, that's what I keep telling myself when I'm feeling down.

Karna You old cynic.

Bror What do you mean? I've been your doting son-in-law for almost fifteen years, and you still don't realize what a gentle, sensitive soul I am.

Karna No? *She carries on crocheting.* And if I couldn't be a lime
tree, I'd be a birch, that's my second favourite. Could you
make sure I'm buried under a lime tree, or if not, a birch?
Magda Mum, what IS wrong with you today?
Karna A birch would do, but definitely not a pine. That's my final
word on the matter, and I mean it, Magda!

Gertrud enters. She walks by, as if she's looking for something.

Gertrud Ulrika called.
Karna *attentively* Ulli?
Gertrud She says hello.
Karna Yes....?
Gertrud Yes what?
Karna Are they coming, then?
Gertrud I don't think so.
Karna But it's my birthday.
Gertrud It was only yesterday you said you didn't want any fuss
on your birthday.
Karna But I say that every year.
Gertrud She said they're getting married.
Karna *very happy* Are they?
Gertrud Yes, but please don't say anything to Tanya.

Gertrud leaves.

Karna *very unhappy* No. Oh I feel terrible about that.
Magda Don't. It's your birthday, remember?

Magda leaves.

Karna *shaking her head* Well, we've all got to go in the end.
That's what you've got to think, whenever you're feeling
miserable.
Bror Yes, what a happy thought. Come on Karna, dear. Cheer up!

Bror leaves. Karna carries on crocheting. Tanya enters. It is not long before the baby's due.

> **Tanya** Frederick's baking you a birthday cake.
> **Karna** He knows I don't like cakes!
> **Tanya** But he enjoys baking them.

Silence. Tanya sits down. She has got back-ache.

> **Tanya** Why don't I ever hear from him?
> **Karna** Who?
> **Tanya** Thomas, of course.
> **Karna** But Tanya, my dear....
> **Tanya** I wrote to him. I want him to be there at the birth, you see. I want him to be there when our son is born.
> **Karna** *after a brief pause* What if it's a girl?
> **Tanya** No, it'll be a boy, and it'll be just like him. I know it.
> **Karna** Tanya, my dear....
> **Tanya** Can I tell you something, Grandma?
> **Karna** Of course you can. No-one ever tells me anything.
> **Tanya** There's no-one else I can tell.
> **Karna** What is it, my dear?
> **Tanya** When I came out here last autumn, well, I was in love with him, you see, and I was hoping he might feel the same way about me. But I didn't know. And then we were together. I knew it wasn't really serious, you know. But he was so nice and gentle. And he liked me. I could feel it. I was so happy.
> **Karna** But Tanya, you knew all about him and Ulli... *Stops.*
> **Tanya** Oh forget it! I won't talk to you if you don't want to listen. Get on with your crocheting, I won't disturb you. *Gets up.*
> **Karna** Tanya, wait! I'm sorry Tanya my dear. It's just I love you all. I'm sorry. There's no right or wrong when it comes to love, and who am I to judge?
> **Tanya** But love can overcome everything, can't it?
> **Karna** Yes, yes, I'm sure it can.

Tanya But their love doesn't mean much, Gran. They argue all the time, him and Ulli. I know they do, Mum told me. *Pause.* You know, I think this winter's never going to end.

Karna Yes, I know.

Tanya I think I've grown up this winter.

Karna Yes.

Tanya And now I know.

Karna Know what?

Tanya That it's him. Him and no-one else.

Karna What do you mean?

Tanya He's the man I love. And he'll love me too, in the end.

Karna *pauses, then, cautiously* It's not always possible to get exactly what you want, Tanya.

Tanya I know.

Karna If you expect too much, you can be disappointed. If you hope for too much, you'll only get hurt. Believe me. I should know.

Tanya What are you trying to say? That I shouldn't hope at all?

Karna I didn't say that.

Tanya No, but that's what you meant, wasn't it? That it's not worth hoping for anything. You're just the same as Frederick and Gertrud and all the others. You don't hope for anything any more. You just go on living. Well I don't want to be like that.

Karna You're right. You can't live without hopes. Just don't build them up too high.

Tanya Somewhere in between, you mean?

Karna Yes....well, no....

Tanya Well, I don't want to be like you lot.

Karna But you don't really think that Thomas and you...? Do you ever see each other?

Tanya How can we! Ulrika wouldn't let him, would she.

Karna How do you know?

Tanya Because she's jealous, isn't she. And because she can't have any children. That's what Mum says. She's probably too old. That's why he can't see me. But I'm having his

child! And one day he'll come back to me, because she won't give him any children.

Karna You think so?

Tanya But don't you dare breathe a word of this to anyone, or I'll strangle you.

Karna Tanya!

Tanya Because they think they own me. But that's where they're wrong, because they don't! No-one does!

Karna *pauses* In a few years time, you'll have forgotten all about him.

Tanya *gets up* No I won't.

Karna But you have to.

Tanya Why?

Karna Because....because they're getting married.

Tanya You're lying! You're lying! *Brief pause.* Anyway, it doesn't matter! They can always get divorced. Everyone does, these days. You did, didn't you. It doesn't matter!

Tanya leaves.

Karna Tanya, wait! Listen to me! Of course you have dreams, but some dreams you just have to give up. I know that only too well. I didn't, and when I finally realized the mistake I'd made, half of my life had wasted away. Tanya, my dear little Tanya. Ulli, my dear Ulli....It's God's punishment, loving as much as I do. But is there anything that's more important? Oh why must everything be so confusing? How are we supposed to be committed to someone one minute, and forget about them the next? To love, and to cherish, then to part, never to see each other again? Every single minute we have to make choices that affect the rest of our lives! But we won't admit it, because if we did, we'd go mad and never make any choices at all. And all this confusion, doesn't it all just boil down to one thing - do we dare risk loving someone and being loved by someone? There must be some other way, some more practical way.

But I've never been practical, all my life. Thank God. Who wants to be practical.

LIGHTS change. Sun is setting. Gertrud and Frederick enter.

Gertrud Mum, did you really have to tell Tanya?
Karna Yes, I did. Don't you think so, Frederick?
Frederick Well, you could have waited a while.
Karna Oh I'm sorry, I'm so sorry.

Magda enters, then Bror.

Magda But she had to be told the truth.
Gertrud But couldn't you have done it a bit more gently?
Frederick I just don't know. But I hate to see her cry. If that bastard dare show his face, I'll shoot him.
Bror 'Writer Murdered by Rifle-wielding Civil Servant.' *Grins.*

They look at each other. Magda tries to hide a smile. Gertrud shrugs her shoulders, begins to put things together, ready to leave. Frederick helps, as does Magda. The sun is setting. Suddenly Thomas and Ulrika appear, with a bunch of flowers for Karna.

Karna *happy* Ulli! Ulrika! Thomas! Dear Thomas!

She hugs them. They all say hello to each other. After a moment's hesitation, Frederick holds out his hand to Thomas.

Ulrika We can only stay for a couple of minutes....we wanted to give Mum some flowers....we always do on her birthday....
Karna If you're getting married, I'd like to be there. *Looks around.* Yes, I know what you're thinking, but I would.
Thomas I'm sorry, but we are already.
Ulrika Maybe we shouldn't have come.

Brief pause.

> **Ulrika** Please try and understand. I'm sorry we came, Gertrud.
> **Gertrud** Ulli. Dear Ulli. Good luck.
> **Ulrika** You really mean that?
> **Gertrud** Yes, yes of course I do....well, no....oh, I don't know.
> **Ulrika** Oh Gertrud.

She rests her head on Gertrud's shoulder. They hug each other. Karna goes over and sits down in her chair, and looks at the sunset over the sea.

> **Karna** Oh, I feel so miserable.
> **Bror** Don't Karna. Look at the sea. Every evening, just as amazing. Far away out there, the water is swallowing the last drops of light. And darkness is falling on the sand, the islands, the clouds....over there, the red buoy by Lundkvist's jetty is disappearing, but the image is still there in your mind. Isn't it a miracle, just being alive on a summer night like this.

The sun sets in the sea. They stand still. Tanya enters. She watches them. They notice her.